FACTS AT YOUR FINGERTIPS

EUROPE

WAYLAND

This edition published in 2008 by Wayland
(a division of Hachette Children's Books)

Wayland
Hachette Children's Books
338 Euston Road
London NW1 3BH

Wayland Australia
Level 17/207 Kent Street
Sydney NSW 2000

© 2008 The Brown Reference Group plc

Brown Bear Books Limited
An imprint of The Brown Reference Group plc
First Floor
9–17 St. Albans Place
London N1 0NX

www.brownreference.com

ISBN-13: 978-0-750256-41-4

Author: Derek Hall
Editorial Director: Lindsey Lowe
Project Director: Graham Bateman
Art Director/Design: Steve McCurdy
Editors: Virginia Carter, Briony Ryles

Printed in Malaysia

Wayland is a division of Hachette Children's Books,
an Hachette Livre UK Company.
www.hachettelivre.co.uk

Picture credits

Cover Images
Front: Moeciu, Romania (Shutterstock/Dumitrescu Ciprian-Florin)

Back: A church bell-tower and windmill, Oia on Santorini/Thira, Greece (Shutterstock/Paul Cowan)

Page 1: Eilean Donan castle, Scotland (Shutterstock/Alfio Ferlito)

All images Shutterstock:
5 Mark Aplet; **6** Laurence Gough; **7** Inozemtcev Konstantin; **8/9** Geir Olav Lyngfjell; **10/11** Aleksandar-Pal Sakala; **12** Jose Antonio Sanchez; **13** Keith Murphy; **14** Artur Bogacki; **16/17** Albert H. Teich; **18** Rui Vale de Sousa; **20/21** Chad Bontrager; **22/23** CJ Photography; **24/25** Christa DeRidder; **26/27** Elisa Locci; **28** Allan Grosskrueger; **29** Nicoleta Bota; **31** Edyta Pawlowska; **32/33** Nathan Jaskowiak; **34/35** Puchan; **36/37** Vinicius Tupinamba; **38** Simon Krzic; **39** Gordana Sermek; **40** Tihis; **41** Milos Markovic; **44** Szabolcs Borbely; **45** Artis Rams; **49** Poznukhov Yuriy; **50/51** Orlov Mihail Anatolevich; **52** Sascha Cristian Maria de Viena; **54/55** Morozova Oksana; **56** Paul Cowan; **58** Ioannis Ioannou; **59** Nick Stubbs; **60/61** Graham Taylor; **61** Michael Schofield.

CONTENTS

EUROPE

Having been battered by two world wars and ripped in half by the Iron Curtain, Europe – previously 'western Europe' and 'eastern Europe' – is now enjoying a period of relative peace and prosperity. The new unified Europe stretches from Portugal and Spain in the southwest to the Urals in the northeast, and from Iceland in the northwest to the shores of the Caspian Sea in the southeast.

Note that this volume includes Siberia, which is a part of the Russian Federation that straddles the continents of both **Europe** and **Asia**.

Early Peoples

When the Egyptians were building pyramids in about 2500 B.C., the peoples of western Europe, although successful farmers, were still erecting relatively crude huts and stone circles. But farther east European civilisation began to flourish, initially under the Greeks (whose empire once extended into Persia), and later under the Romans (occupiers of France and Britain).

After the Roman Empire collapsed, the Celts, who had occupied much of mainland Europe, were pushed back to its western fringes by the Germanic Angles, Saxons and Jutes. Celtic influence remains to this day, in Brittany (in France), in Cornwall (in England) and in Wales, Ireland and Scotland. Other peoples included the Normans (noted for church architecture) and the Vikings (the first Europeans to reach North America).

Colonial History

Europe's more recent colonial history has been one of expansion and conquest. Britain, Spain, France and Portugal colonised the Americas. The same nations – along with the Dutch, Germans and Belgians – looked to Africa. The Indian subcontinent was 'British', Indo-China was 'French' and Indonesia was once known as the Dutch East Indies.

The colonial process has now been reversed, and western Europe has become a multicultural, multiracial society. Peoples from the Caribbean (whose ancestors were likely to have been slaves) and Pakistan have settled in Britain, as have Africans in France.

Today's Europe

Although Europe still has a strong manufacturing base, industries and jobs are increasingly relocating to China and elsewhere in Asia. Agriculture and fishing remain but have had to adapt, not just to changing tastes and to overfishing, but to comply with European law.

The City of London is the largest of many financial centres, European banks are some of the largest and most profitable in the world, and both the North Sea and Russia have yielded deposits of oil and natural gas. Tourism, too, is important to the economy and seems destined to become a growth area now that the former Iron Curtain countries have been opened up and, in many cases, admitted to the European Union (EU).

There was a time when the main religions tended to be either Christianity in the west and north or Islam in the east, but such neat geographical boundaries have become increasingly meaningless. This is partly because of the movement of peoples following the introduction and subsequent expansion of the EU and partly due to immigration – for example, from the Caribbean and the Indian subcontinent into Britain, from Africa into France and from Turkey into Germany.

Natural Europe

Despite lying on a line of latitude five degrees to the north of Quebec City, southern England sees very little snow. This is because most of western Europe lies within a temperate zone warmed by the Gulf Stream.

Main geographical features include mountains such as the Pyrenees and the Alps, Norway's fjords, the Rhine and Danube Rivers, the Mediterranean Sea, the lakes of Finland, the sheer cliffs on the Atlantic coast of Ireland, the volcanoes of southern Italy and Iceland and the Black Sea coast of the former Soviet Union.

In the more remote, more northerly areas of Scandinavia, animal life includes caribou ('reindeer' in Europe), bears, wolves and moose ('elk' in Europe).

Shingle-tiled rooftops with dormer windows reflect the autumn sun. Such architecture is a common sight not only in many parts of Europe but also in former colonies abroad.

ICELAND

The island republic of Iceland lies just below the Arctic Circle. It is a volcanically active region where earth tremors are frequent and hot springs are a common sight, especially at Geysir in the southwest. Similar springs gave the capital its name – Reykjavik, or 'Smoky Bay' – and today they provide most of the country's hot water and heating. At the heart of the island is a high plateau, partly covered by a glacier and surrounded by mountains. Glaciers account for over one-tenth of Iceland's surface area. Steep valleys are found in the north. Temperatures are above average for this latitude, thanks to warm southwesterly winds associated with the North Atlantic Drift. Rainfall is high throughout the year. The original woodland was cleared by settlers, and shrubs, mosses and lichens now predominate. Bird life is rich and varied, especially on sea cliffs.

The first settlers were probably Irish monks, followed in about 870 A.D. by Vikings. Today most of the population lives on the narrow coastal plain around Reykjavik. Iceland was an important Allied base during World War II, and since 1951 a U.S. military presence has been established at Keflavík. Along with Iceland's membership of NATO, this is a hotly debated issue.

The cornerstone of the economy is fishing, which accounts for three-quarters of exports. There are also more than 4,500 farms in Iceland, engaged in livestock grazing and vegetable and flower production. Food processing, software production, biotechnology, tourism and financial services are also important industries.

A geothermal power station. A cheap and abundant source of fuel, it powers many of the island's industries, as well as providing heating for domestic and commercial use.

NATIONAL DATA – ICELAND

Land area	100,250 sq km (38,707 sq mi)			

Climate		Temperatures		Annual
	Altitude m (ft)	January °C (°F)	July °C (°F)	precipitation mm (in)
Reykjavik	52 (170)	0 (32)	11 (52)	817 (32)

Major physical features highest point: Hvannadalshnúkur 2,119 m (6,952 ft); longest river: Thjórsà 230 km (143 mi)

Population (2006 est.) 299,388

Form of government multiparty republic with one legislative house

Armed forces paramilitary 130

Capital city Reykjavik (184,244)

Official language Icelandic

Ethnic composition Icelandic 96.4%; other Europeans 2.5%; Asian 0.7%; others 0.4%

Religious affiliations Lutheran 85.5%; Reykjavik Free Church 2.1%; Roman Catholic 2%; Hafnarfjorour Free Church 1.5%; other Christian 2.7%; other or unspecified 3.8%; unaffiliated 2.4%

Currency 1 Icelandic króna (ISK) = 100 aurar

Gross domestic product (2006) U.S. $11.4 billion

Gross domestic product per capita (2006.) U.S. $38,100

Life expectancy at birth male 78.23 yr; female 82.48 yr

Major resources cattle, dairy products, diatomite, fish, fodder, hay, hydroelectric and geothermal power, potatoes, poultry, sheep

FINLAND

NATIONAL DATA – FINLAND

Land area	338,145 sq km (130,559 sq mi)			

Climate		Temperatures		Annual
	Altitude m (ft)	January °C (°F)	July °C (°F)	precipitation mm (in)
Helsinki	51 (167)	-6 (21)	17 (63)	635.4 (25)

Major physical features highest point: Haltiatunturi (northern Finland) 1,328 m (4,357 ft); longest river: Kemi 548 km (343 mi); largest lake: Lake Saimaa 1,147 sq km (443 sq mi)

Population (2006 est.) 5,231,372

Form of government multiparty republic with one legislative house

Armed forces army 1,920; navy 5,000; air force 2,800

Largest cities Helsinki (capital – 559,046); Espoo (231,704); Tampere (202,932)

Official language Finnish, Swedish

Ethnic composition Finn 93.4%; Swede 5.7%; Russian 0.4%; Estonian 0.2%; Roma 0.2%; Sami 0.1%

Religious affiliations Lutheran National Church 84.2%; Greek Orthodox in Finland 1.1%; other Christian 1.1%; other 0.1%; none 13.5%

Currency 1 euro (EUR) = 100 euro cents

Gross domestic product (2006) U.S. $171.7 billion

Gross domestic product per capita (2006) U.S. $32,800

Life expectancy at birth male 74.99 yr; female 82.17 yr

Major resources timber, iron ore, copper, lead, zinc, chromite, nickel, gold, silver, limestone, cereals, dairy products, fish, livestock, potatoes

A view of Karelia in eastern Finland. The country is mainly low-lying, with more than 60,000 lakes and many rivers. The local name for the country, Suomi, means 'land of lakes and marshes'.

Finland is Europe's sixth largest country, and one-third of its land lies within the Arctic Circle. The autonomous Åland Islands off the southwestern coast are an extension of the coastal lowland; some 80 of the 3,000 islands in the archipelago are inhabited. Apart from a hilly region in the northeast, Finland is low-lying, with many lakes connected by an extensive river system. Most of the country is forested and inhabited by animals such as bears, lynx, elks and wolves. The rivers abound with salmon, trout and waterfowl. As in other Nordic countries, there is evidence of environmental damage caused by acid rain, and radiation from the 1986 Chernobyl disaster still affects reindeer herds.

During the Cold War Finland steered a delicate course, maintaining its democratic tradition alongside its giant communist neighbor, the Soviet Union. The country became a member of the EU in 1995. The economy today is largely based on its major resource, timber, which accounts for over one-third of exports. About 9 percent of the land is cultivated, with most farms being smallholdings combining crop rearing with forestry. Manufacturing and other industries account for a quarter of the country's income, with hydroelectricity and nuclear power providing the bulk of the energy.

NORWAY

Norway lies on the western coast of the Scandinavian peninsula. Long and thin – just 80 km (50 mi) across at its narrowest point and 450 km (280 mi) across at its widest – the country is a rugged land that supports only a small population. Norway includes the desolate Arctic Ocean islands of Svalbard and Jan Mayen.

NATIONAL DATA – NORWAY

Land area 307,442 sq km (118,673 sq mi)

Climate	Altitude	Temperatures		Annual precipitation
	m (ft)	January °C (°F)	July °C (°F)	mm (in)
Oslo	96 (314)	–4 (24)	17 (62)	655 (26)
Bergen	39 (127)	1 (34)	14 (58)	2,074 (82)

Major physical features highest point: Galdhøpiggen 2,469 m (8,100 ft); longest river: Glåma 611 km (380 mi)

Population (2006 est.) 4,610,820

Form of government multiparty constitutional monarchy with one legislative house

Armed forces army 14,700; navy 5,310; air force 5,000

Largest cities Oslo (capital – 521,886); Bergen (237,430); Trondheim (154,351)

Official language Norwegian

Ethnic composition Norwegian 95.8%; other Scandinavians 1.0%; others 3.2%

Religious affiliations Church of Norway 85.7%; Pentecostal 1%; Roman Catholic 1%; other Christian 2.4%; Muslim 1.8%; other 8.1%

Currency 1 Norwegian krone (NOK) = 100 øre

Gross domestic product (2006) U.S. $207.3 billion

Gross domestic product per capita (2006) U.S. $47,800

Life expectancy at birth male 76.91 yr; female 82.31 yr

Major resources petroleum, natural gas, iron ore, copper, lead, zinc, pyrites, nickel, fish, timber, hydropower, apples, barley, coal, livestock, oats, potatoes, silicon, titanium

Geography

Norway's ancient granite rocks were eroded by ice-age glaciers and shaped into high mountains and deep valleys. The country has more than 160,000 lakes, and fjords (high-walled sea lakes in glacial valleys) turn the coastline into a maze flanked by some 50,000 islands.

Glacial erosion has flattened some mountains, creating huge plateaus such as Hardangervidda in southern central Norway. Farther north is the Jotunheimen mountain range, and towards the coast is the Jostedalsbreen ice field. Northern Norway, within the Arctic Circle, ends in the Finnmark Plateau. There are important lowland farming areas in the southeast, around Oslo, the Trøndelag in central Norway and near Stavanger in the southwest. Below the Arctic Circle, the North Atlantic Drift gives western Norway a temperate climate. Eastern

Norway has colder winters, warmer summers and lower rainfall. About one-quarter of the country is forested. Other vegetation includes Scandinavian delicacies such as blueberries, cranberries and cloudberries. However, acid rain caused by industrial air pollution originating in neighbouring countries has damaged large areas.

Society

Huge mountains and deep fjords have always made travel and communication by land difficult, and Norway is a country with a long maritime tradition. The earliest settlers were hunter-gatherers from central Europe, but by the 9th century A.D. settled farming was well established. Settlers then began trading and raiding in places such as England and northern France. They also settled in Greenland and Iceland, and crossed the Atlantic to North America. (The name Viking comes from Skagerrak, the strait between Norway and Denmark, then called Vik.) Following union with Sweden in 1814, Norway gained independence in 1905. During World War II Norway was occupied by Germany from 1940 to 1945. Norway is a member of NATO.

Fishing boats moored against the stark backdrop of Norway's mountainous fjords. The country's fishing fleet has been reduced by a quarter as a result of overfishing by international fleets.

Norway's cultural history is long and distinguished. Famous figures include the composer Edvard Grieg (1843–1907) and the painter Edvard Munch (1863–1944). Notable scientist-explorers include Fridtjof Nansen (1861–1930) and Thor Heyerdahl (1914–2002).

Economy

The difficult climate and terrain mean that only 5 percent of Norway's land can be farmed, and so the economy is largely industrial. Almost half of the southern coastal agricultural area provides pasture; the rest is used to grow cereals, potatoes and animal fodder. Forestry and fishing, the major agricultural earners, are heavily subsidised by the government.

Metallic ores are mined on the mainland. Iron and steel production have now been replaced by aluminum production from imported bauxite. Norway continues to be a leading exporter of nickel, copper and zinc. In the 1970s natural gas and oil deposits were found in the Norwegian North Sea sector, and the country became a significant oil and gas exporter, but other industries suffered from lack of investment. The oil-dependent economy suffered from fluctuating oil prices in the late 1970s and 1980s, and today much of Norway's energy is produced by hydroelectric plants on the many fast-flowing rivers. The fishing fleet, although declining, still contributes greatly to the balance of payments.

TRANSPORT IN NORWAY

Norway's difficult terrain means that coastal shipping is still the main means of transporting goods around. There are busy ports around the coast at Oslo, Narvik, Trondheim, Bergen and Stavanger. Overland transportation is heavily subsidised. The rail network links Oslo with Stavanger and Bergen. A railway line extends to Trondheim, but the rail link to Narvik in the north is via Sweden. About two-thirds of the road system is surfaced, and bus transport (with linked ferry services) is important in remote areas. There is also a 1,577-km (980-mi) waterways network along the west coast. There are more than 40 local airfields, and international airports at Oslo, Stavanger and Bergen.

SWEDEN

Sweden is the fourth largest totally European country. Its people enjoy a very high standard of living, a highly developed welfare system and one of the highest average incomes in the world. Sweden takes a strongly independent approach to world affairs.

NATIONAL DATA – SWEDEN

Land area   410,934 sq km (158,663 sq mi)

Climate		Temperatures		Annual
	Altitude m (ft)	January °C (°F)	July °C (°F)	precipitation mm (in)
Stockholm	52 (170)	-3.5 (25.7)	17 (63)	502 (20)

Major physical features   highest point: Kebnekaise 2,111 m (6,926 ft); longest river: Göta-Klar 715 km (447 mi); largest lake: Lake Vänern 5,584 sq km (2,156 sq mi)

Population   (2006 est.) 9,016,596

Form of government   multiparty constitutional monarchy with one legislative house

Armed forces   army 13,800; navy 7,900; air force 5,900

Largest cities   Stockholm (capital – 1,889,945); Göteborg (481,410); Malmö (271,271)

Official language   Swedish

Ethnic composition   Swedish 88.5%; Finnish 2.2%; other Europeans 4.7%; Asians 3%; other 1.6%

Religious affiliations   Lutheran 86.5% (non practicing 30.0%); Muslim 2.3% Roman Catholic 1.8%; Pentecostal 1.1%; others 8.3%

Currency   1 Swedish krona (SEK) = 100 öre

Gross domestic product   (2006) U.S. $285.1 billion

Gross domestic product per capita   (2006) U.S. $31,600

Life expectancy at birth   male 78.29 yr; female 82.87 yr

Major resources   iron ore, copper, lead, zinc, gold, silver, tungsten, coal, uranium, arsenic, feldspar, timber, hydropower, cereals, dairy products, potatoes, rape seed, sugar beet

Geography

Sweden can be divided into two parts. The northern mountains and plateaus account for two-thirds of the land area; they are thickly forested and rich in minerals. Most of Sweden's large rivers flow from the plateaus towards the coastal plains along the Gulf of Bothnia. The southern lowlands contain four-fifths of the population and most of the agricultural land and manufacturing industries. This region has many lakes. The Baltic coastline is rocky, with numerous small islands.

Extending north into the Arctic Circle and south to the same latitude as Copenhagen, Denmark, Sweden has a varied climate. The north and east are influenced by cold Arctic conditions, while the south benefits from

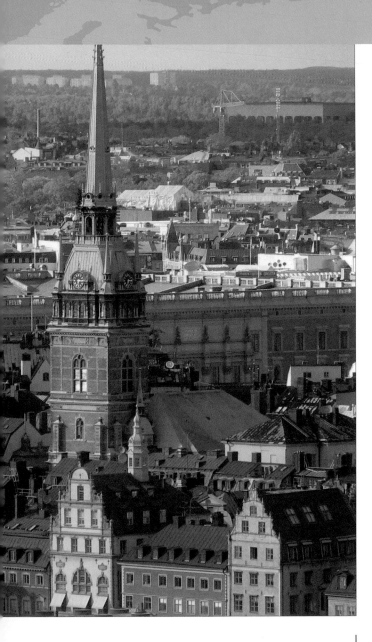

Faroese. The largest ethnic minority (some 17,000 people) are the Sami, who have a distinct language and culture. Sweden became a member of the EU in 1995.

Economy

The prime natural resources of Sweden are lumber, iron ore and water – which is used for hydroelectric power. All three resources are largely confined to Norrland, the mountainous region in the north and centre of the country. Forestry and engineering have been the chief export earners since the collapse of the ship-building industry. About 60 percent of the total land area is devoted to forestry, which yields turpentine, resins, dyes, rayon and plastics as well as wood pulp and paper. Less than 7 percent of the land is farmed, but it meets four-fifths of the domestic needs. About 3 percent of the population is employed in the industry. Crops include sugar beet, barley, potatoes and wheat. Other farming produce includes livestock and fur. Fishing makes only a small contribution to the economy.

Kiruna in northern Norrland has an extremely rich iron ore deposit, and a processing plant has been built at Luleå on the Bothnian coast. Other minerals include precious metals, copper, zinc and coal. Manufacturing ranges from transport equipment and machinery to electronic and telecommunications hardware.

The skyline of Stockholm, the capital and largest city. Increasing mechanisation and rationalisation of farms are causing a rural exodus; about 83 percent of Swedes now live in towns and cities.

warm winds brought by the North Atlantic Drift, producing mild, wet winters and cool summers.

Deciduous woodlands in the southwest give way to pine and spruce farther north and at higher elevations, while alpine vegetation grows on the mountains. Bears and lynx are restricted to northern forests, and other mammals include wolves, foxes, deer, hares, otters and seals. The Sami (Lapps) keep herds of domesticated reindeer. Bird life is rich and varied.

Society

Sweden's political, social and cultural history is closely linked to other Scandinavian countries. The Swedish language is closely related to Norwegian, Icelandic and

CARED FOR BY THE STATE

Since World War II, Sweden's predominantly socialist governments have provided ample welfare provisions for its citizens, brought about through high taxation. Virtually everyone is provided with child allowances, pensions for old age and disability and benefits for sickness, maternity and unemployment. Medical fees are largely paid for by the state. Everyone is entitled to continue their studies after leaving school, to prepare for university or vocational training. Adult education is also available. Distance or home learning is available with support from radio, TV, or correspondence courses.

DENMARK

Denmark is the smallest country in Scandinavia. The mainland, the Jutland Peninsula, extends 300 km (200 mi) north from the border with Germany. Lagoons, sandbars and dunes shelter the west coast from North Sea storms. The eastern plains face the Baltic Sea and an archipelago of 483 islands, of which 97 are settled.

Progressive, but deeply interested in their past, the Danes have achieved a healthy and equitable society.

They enjoy perhaps the highest standard of living in the EU, with an extensive welfare program. Farming accounts for two-thirds of the land area, but it employs only one-sixteenth of the workforce. About half the country's farm produce is exported within the EU; in fact, Denmark trades almost entirely within Europe. The food-processing industry is the second largest employer. The country also has a large fishing industry which is among the world's top 15.

Mineral resources are heavily exploited. North Sea gas and oil supply half of Denmark's energy, and wind turbines are increasingly common in flat, windy Jutland. Industrial products include cement, machinery, electronics and brewing.

NATIONAL DATA – DENMARK

| Land area   42,394 sq km (16,368 sq mi) |

Climate		Temperatures		Annual
	Altitude m (ft)	January °C (°F)	July °C (°F)	precipitation mm (in)
Copenhagen	9 (30)	0 (32)	17 (63)	587 (23)

Major physical features   highest point: Yding Skovhøj (central Jutland) 173 m (568 ft); largest island: Sjaelland 7,016 sq km (2,709 sq mi)

Population   (2006 est.) 5,450,661

Form of government   multiparty constitutional monarchy with one legislative house

Armed forces   army 12,500; navy 3,800; air force 4,200

Largest cities   Copenhagen (capital – 1,086,762); Arhus (228,547); Odense (145,554); Alborg (121,549)

Official language   Danish

Ethnic composition   Danish 95.1%; other European 1.5%; Asian 1.3%; other 2.1%

Religious affiliations   Evangelical Lutheran 95%; other Protestant and Roman Catholic 3%; Muslim 2%

Currency   1 Danish krone (DKK) = 100 øre

Gross domestic product   (2006) U.S. $198.5 billion

Gross domestic product per capita   (2006) U.S. $37,000

Life expectancy at birth   male 75.49 yr; female 80.22 yr

Major resources   petroleum, natural gas, fish, salt, limestone, chalk, stone, gravel, sand, electronics, textiles, cattle, cereals, coal, cryolite, fodder, iron ore, lead, molybdenum, natural gas, pigs, potatoes, poultry, uranium, zinc

Nyhavn, part of the original Copenhagen harbor, is a popular and vibrant area. It attracts visitors with its fascinating old ships and buildings and its many places to eat and drink.

IRELAND

The Republic of Ireland, or Eire, occupies some five-sixths of the island of Ireland, located about 80 km (50 mi) off the west coast of Great Britain. Known as 'the Emerald Isle' because of its lush green landscapes, Ireland is surrounded by a broken rim of mountains. The low-lying central plain has many lakes (or loughs), bogs and broad rivers. The Shannon is the longest river in the British Isles. The coastline in the west is rocky and indented, with spectacular cliffs. Mild Atlantic winds bring frequent rain. Peat bogs carpet much of central Ireland. Long used as a source of domestic fuel, the bogs – habitats for rare plants – are now threatened by the use of peat in power stations and in horticulture.

Ireland's history is one of turmoil, bloodshed, religious conflict, continuous emigration and the fight for independence. Today it is a stable democracy with a strong musical and literary tradition. Famous writers include Jonathan Swift (1667–1745), Oscar Wilde (1854–1900) and Samuel Beckett (1906–91).

Agriculture employs about 10 percent of the workforce, mainly on owner-occupied smallholdings. Sea fisheries were modernised in the 1970s, but are subject to overfishing controls. As well as peat, offshore oil and gas reserves help meet the country's fuel needs. The industrial sector accounts for about 40 percent of GDP, and manufacturing has increased strongly, especially in chemicals, computers and software. The financial sector has also expanded greatly. The service sector now accounts for over 60 percent of employment. Economic growth in the past decade has been robust.

NATIONAL DATA - IRELAND

Land area	68,890 sq km (26,599 sq mi)			
Climate		Temperatures	Annual	
	Altitude m (ft)	January °C (°F)	July °C (°F)	precipitation mm (in)
Dublin	81 (266)	5 (41)	15 (59)	733 (28.8)

Major physical features highest point: Carrauntoohill (Macgillicuddy's Reeks) 1,041 m (3,414 ft); longest river: Shannon 370 km (230 mi)

Population (2006 est.) 4,062,235

Form of government multiparty republic with two legislative houses

Armed forces army 8,500; navy 1,100; air force 860

Largest cities Dublin (capital - 1,186,159); Cork (119,143); Galway (65,832); Limerick (54,023); Waterford (44,594)

Official language Irish, English

Ethnic composition Irish 95%; British 2.7%; others 2.3%

Religious affiliations Roman Catholic 88.4%; Church of Ireland 3%; other Christian 1.6%; other 1.5%; unspecified 2%; none 3.5%

Currency 1 Euro (EUR) = 100 euro cents

Gross domestic product (2006) U.S. $177.2 billion

Gross domestic product per capita (2006) U.S. $43,600

Life expectancy at birth male 75.11 yr; female 80.52 yr

Major resources natural gas, peat, copper, lead, zinc, silver, barite, gypsum, limestone, dolomite, barytes, cereals, fish, livestock, potatoes, sugar beet, vegetables, tourism

The pub is a vital part of Irish social life and culture. Many small towns boast a dozen or more licenced establishments. Many ordinary retailers even provide 'bar' facilities for thirsty shoppers.

UNITED KINGDOM

The United Kingdom lies off the Atlantic northwest coast of continental Europe, to which it was once joined. The United Kingdom consists of the countries of England, Scotland and Wales (collectively known as Great Britain) together with the six counties of Northern Ireland. Each country within the United Kingdom has its own distinct culture and identity.

NATIONAL DATA – UNITED KINGDOM

Land area 241,590 sq km (93,278 sq mi)

Climate		Temperatures		Annual
	Altitude m (ft)	January °C (°F)	July °C (°F)	precipitation mm (in)
London	7 (22)	4 (39)	17 (63)	611 (24)

Major physical features highest point: Ben Nevis 1,343 m (4,406 ft); lowest point: Holme Fen (The Fens) –4 m (–13 ft); longest river: Severn 290 km (180 mi)

Population (2006 est.) 60,609,153

Form of government multiparty constitutional monarchy with two legislative houses

Armed forces army 117,300; navy 40,700; air force 48,585

Largest cities London (capital – 7,172,091); Birmingham (989,141); Leeds (715,402); Glasgow (629,501); Sheffield (513,234); Edinburgh (452,194); Liverpool (439,473); Manchester (395,323); Bristol (380,615); Cardiff (305,353); Belfast (277,391)

Official language English

Ethnic composition White (English 83.6%; Scottish 8.6%; Welsh 4.9%; Northern Irish 2.9%) 92.1%; Black 2%; Indian 1.8%; Pakistani 1.3%; Mixed 1.2%; other 1.6%

Religious affiliations Christian (Anglican, Roman Catholic, Presbyterian, Methodist) 71.6%; Muslim 2.7%; Hindu 1%; other 1.1%; unspecified or none 23.6%

Currency 1 pound sterling (GBP) = 100 pence

Gross domestic product (2006) U.S. $1.903 trillion

Gross domestic product per capita (2006) U.S. $31,400

Life expectancy at birth male 76.09 yr; female 81.13 yr

Major resources coal, petroleum, natural gas, iron ore, lead, zinc, tin, limestone, salt, clay, chalk, gypsum, potash, silica sand, slate, barley, fruit, vegetables, fish, potatoes, sugar beet, wheat, tourism

Geography

A fairly small land area contains great diversity of landscape and geology, with numerous mountain ranges, lakes, rivers and varied coastlines. Much of southern and central England has gently rolling countryside, flatter in the east. Northern England, Scotland, Wales and Northern Ireland have a high proportion of rugged terrain and mountains. Ben Nevis, the highest peak in the United Kingdom, is in the western Scottish Highlands. Despite the northerly latitude, the climate is generally mild, although high winds and heavy rain are common.

Once heavily wooded, the land is now mainly moorland in the northern uplands and farmland in the south and lowlands, with smaller areas of managed deciduous and conifer woodland in places. A rich variety of animal and plant life exists, however.

Society

European settlers first arrived here across an ice-age land bridge that later disappeared. Since then Romans, Vikings and Normans have been among those who have influenced Britain's long and colourful history. From 1945, immigration from Commonwealth countries began to create a multicultural and multiracial society.

With nearly 1,000 years of unbroken royal descent, the British Isles were the birthplace of modern parliamentary democracy, of the Industrial Revolution, and of the welfare state. The English language is spoken by 350 million people worldwide. Another billion people use English as a second language.

Unconquered since 1066, the United Kingdom faces new constitutional challenges in the form of an increasingly federal Europe and national assemblies in Wales, Scotland and Northern Ireland, as well as rapid changes in the composition of its population caused by large-scale immigration. Less than 10 percent of the population now lives in rural areas. The United Kingdom continues to play an influential role in world affairs.

Lincoln Cathedral, England. This fine example of a Gothic style cathedral is one of many built around England in the middle ages.

ISLANDS OF THE UNITED KINGDOM

Around the mainland, many islands bear witness to the United Kingdom's historic legacy. The self-governing Channel Islands have been dependencies of the British crown since 1066; they were the only British territory occupied by Nazi Germany in World War II. The Isle of Man is another crown possession that is virtually self-governing, coming under British control in the 15th century. Farther north, the western isles of Scotland are indelibly etched with the romantic tale of Charles Edward Stuart, 'Bonnie Prince Charlie', a claimant to the British throne who escaped the English forces by perilous sea crossings to Uist, and then Skye, in 1746. (See also pages 60–61).

Economy

Britain's early industrial superiority was diminished in the 20th century by the breakup of its empire and the economic costs of two world wars. It was also undermined by increasing foreign competition. Since 1945 the most significant developments have been the exploitation of North Sea oil and gas reserves, changing patterns of trade within the EU, and the shift towards a service-based economy.

Farming is highly mechanised, and agriculture supplies about half the demand for food but employs only 1 percent of the workforce. Fishing is in decline through overfishing, EU restrictions, and foreign competition, but fish farming is increasing. Britain's limited minerals have been heavily depleted, and most of the coal now used is in the form of cheaper imports. Natural oil and gas, together with nuclear power, provide much of the energy requirements. Manufactured goods include steel, motor vehicles, aerospace equipment, electrical goods, electronics, chemicals and textiles. The service sector, telecommunications and financial services are other important industries. The transport system is well developed but severely overcrowded.

SCOTLAND

NORTHERN IRELAND

WALES   ENGLAND

SPAIN

Spain occupies the greater part of the Iberian Peninsula, between the Atlantic Ocean and the Mediterranean Sea. The autonomous Balearic Islands in the western Mediterranean and Canary Islands off the Atlantic coast of Africa are also administered by Spain.

NATIONAL DATA – SPAIN

Land area 499,542 sq km (192,874 sq mi)

Climate	Altitude m (ft)	Temperatures January °C (°F)	July °C (°F)	Annual precipitation mm (in)
Santander	64 (210)	10 (50)	19 (66)	1,095 (43)
Madrid	609 (1.998)	5 (42)	25 (76)	437 (17.2)
Seville	13 (43)	11 (52)	27 (81)	533 (20.9)

Major physical features highest point: (mainland) Mulhacén 3,481 m (11,421 ft); (Canaries) Pico de Teide 3,715 m (12,188 ft); longest river: Tagus (part) 1,007 km (626 mi)

Population (2006 est.) 40,397,842

Form of government multiparty republic with two legislative houses

Armed forces army 95,600; navy 19,455; air force 22,750

Largest cities Madrid (capital – 3,092,759); Barcelona (1,578,546); Valencia (785,732); Sevilla (704,154); Zaragoza (638,799); Malaga (558,287)

Official language Castillian Spanish

Ethnic composition Spanish 44.9%; Catalan 28%; Galician 8.2%; Basque 5.5%; Aragonese 5%; Roma 2%; others 6.4%

Religious affiliations Roman Catholic 92%; Muslim 0.5%; Protestant 0.3%; other 7.2%

Currency 1 euro (EUR) = 100 euro cents

Gross domestic product (2006) U.S. $1.07 trillion

Gross domestic product per capita (2006) U.S. $27,000

Life expectancy at birth male 76.32 yr; female 83.2 yr

Major resources coal, lignite, iron ore, copper, lead, zinc, uranium, pyrites, mercury, tungsten, magnesite, fluorspar, gypsum, sepiolite, kaolin, potash, hydropower, almonds, cereals, cork, cotton, fruit, fish, grapes/wine, olives, sugar cane, leather, timber, tin, tobacco, vegetables, tourism

Geography

Spain's landscape is dominated by the Meseta, a huge central plateau of ancient rock that covers more than half the country. Largely dry and treeless, it has an average elevation of about 600 m (2,000 ft). The Meseta is surrounded by mountain ranges such as the Cordillera Cantábrica in the northwest, the Pyrenees in the northeast, and the Sierra Morena in the south. The Sierra Nevada range in southern Spain contains the highest mountain on the Iberian Peninsula, Mulhacén. The Meseta is drained by the rivers Douro and Tagus. The Guadalquivir River irrigates the southern plains.

Spain's Mediterranean climate is modified by westerly North Atlantic winds and warm, dry air from the Sahara. The northern zone has mild winters and cool summers. Along the eastern and southern coasts a Mediterranean climate prevails, with mild winters and warm, dry summers. Deciduous forest is found in the humid north, with coniferous forests in the south. Some southern parts have subtropical vegetation. The Meseta is covered in sparse scrub. Grass steppe known as *esparto* grows in the arid southeast. Spain lies on a major bird migration route between Europe and Africa.

Society

Romans, Visigoths, Moors and other invaders have left their diverse marks on Spanish history. From the 15th century the country was a major power, with an empire in Central and South America and parts of Asia. It is interesting to reflect that this most modern and vibrant of European countries was, from the 1930s to the late 1970s, governed by a fascist dictatorship. In spite of ethnic uniformity, Spain today has sharp regional differences in language, local custom and culinary tastes. The most notably distinct are the Basque country in the northwest and Catalonia in the northeast.

Economy

Spain's mainly agricultural economy was transformed by rapid economic growth after the mid–1950s, stimulated by the rationalisation of major industries. Even so, imports normally exceed exports, and tourism (the main industry on the Mediterranean coast) is vital to Spain's balance of trade. Most arable

The 16th-century cathedral towers over the ancient city of Segovia, which is located on a high, rocky spur in central Spain.

land is on the Meseta, and barley and wheat are the main cereal crops, with fruit-growing also widespread. Fishing is mainly confined to the Atlantic coasts, and catches include sardines, anchovies, cod and hake. Spain has a few minerals, but relies heavily on imported petroleum. Nuclear power provides about one-third of energy needs. Several multinational automobile companies have plants in Spain, and there is a large oil-refining industry at Algeciras. Ceramics and handicrafts such as leather, glassworks and metalwork are also important to the economy. Spain is a member of the EU.

PORTUGAL

Occupying the western side of the Iberian Peninsula, Portugal's territories include the Atlantic islands of Madeira and the Azores. Portugal falls into two main geographical regions, divided by the Tagus River. The lusher, more mountainous north contrasts with the drier lowland areas of the south. The Mediterranean climate is influenced by sea and landscape. Winters are cool and wet. Summers on the coast are humid, but summers in the interior are hot and dry. Portugal has forests in the north. The south is less wooded, but the Algarve is famous for its groves of carob, fig and almond trees. Mammals (including bears and wolves), reptiles and birds (some unique to Iberia) are plentiful.

Portugal's predominantly agricultural economy has a relatively low output, because farms have not been modernised. Fruit crops include figs and olives. Wine is the major agricultural export, along with tomatoes and cork. There is commercial fishing along the Atlantic coast. Portugal has few energy reserves. Small amounts of copper pyrites and kaolin are exported, and larger amounts of tungsten ore. Heavy industry, which is concentrated around Lisbon's shipyards, has suffered from falling demand. Fish canning, tobacco processing, footwear, textiles and paper are the main light industries. Tourism is growing fast, especially around the Algarve. Portugal trades chiefly with its EU partners.

Oporto, Portugal's bustling second city, is the commercial hub of the northern industrial heartland.

NATIONAL DATA – PORTUGAL

Land area	91,951 sq km (35,493 sq mi)			

Climate		Temperatures		Annual
	Altitude m (ft)	January °C (°F)	July °C (°F)	precipitation mm (in)
Lisbon	77 (252)	11 (51)	22 (71)	702 (27)

Major physical features highest point: (mainland) Estrela (Serra de Estrela) 1,991 m (6,532 ft); (Azores) Ponta do Pico 2,351 m (7,713 ft); longest river: Tagus (part) 1,007 km (626 mi)

Population (2006 est.) 10,605,870

Form of government multiparty republic with one legislative house

Armed forces army 26,700; navy 10,950; air force 7,250

Largest cities Lisbon (capital – 1,977,000); Oporto (1,303,000)

Official language Portuguese

Ethnic composition Portuguese 91.9%; African 1.6%; Brazilian 1.4%; others 5.1%

Religious affiliations Roman Catholic 87.4%; other Christian 3.7%; Protestant 1.3%; others 1.1%; nonreligious 6.5%

Currency 1 euro (EUR) = 1 euro cent

Gross domestic product (2006) U.S. $203.1 billion

Gross domestic product per capita (2006) U.S. $19,100

Life expectancy at birth male 74.43 yr; female 81.2 yr

Major resources fish, cork, iron ore, copper, zinc, tin, tungsten, silver, gold, uranium, marble, clay, gypsum, salt, hydropower, cereals, citrus fruits, figs, vegetables, fish, grapes/wine, olives, rice, timber, tourism

ANDORRA

The tiny principality of Andorra has a rugged landscape, with high peaks towering above steep valleys and gorges. The joint heads of state are the President of France and the Bishop of Urgel, but they can only veto matters that affect the borders of France and Spain. Andorra depends on France and Spain for defense, its communications network and its education system. Commercial agriculture is very limited owing to the high mountains and alpine climate, but in recent years Andorra has taken advantage of its architecture, scenery and winter climate – as well as its duty-free consumer goods – to promote tourism, especially skiing. Its banking and services have also grown rapidly.

NATIONAL DATA – ANDORRA

Land area 464 sq km (179 sq mi)

Climate		Temperatures		Annual
	Altitude m (ft)	January °C (°F)	July °C (°F)	precipitation mm (in)
Andorra la Vella	1,080 (3,543)	2 (36)	19 (67)	808 (31.8)

Major physical features highest point: Coma Pedrosa 2,946 m (9,665 ft)

Population (2006 est.) 71,201

Form of government parliamentary democracy with one legislative house

Armed forces no armed forces

Largest cities Andorra la Vella (22,035)

Official language Catalan

Ethnic composition Spanish 38%; Andorran 37%; Portuguese 11.5; French 6%; others 13.5%

Religious affiliations Roman Catholic 89.1%; other Christian 4.3%; other 1.6%; nonreligious 5%

Currency 1 euro (EUR) = 100 euro cents

Gross domestic product (2004) U.S. $1.84 billion

Gross domestic product per capita (2004) U.S. $24,000

Life expectancy at birth male 80.61 yr; female 86.61 yr

Major resources hydropower, mineral water, timber, iron ore, lead, barley, cattle, potatoes, rye, sheep, tobacco, vegetables, tourism

MONACO

Monaco, a fashionable resort on the Mediterranean coast, is world-famous for its casinos and its glittering productions of opera and ballet. The densely populated principality also hosts two international motor racing events – the Monte Carlo Rally and the Monaco Grand Prix. The Grimaldi family has ruled Monaco since 1297, with a break in 1793 when the country was declared a republic. The family was restored to power in 1815. Since 1964 Monaco's area has increased by over 20 percent thanks to reclamation of land from the sea. The economy depends largely on financial services, but there is also a thriving tourism sector. The economy has diversified to include a number of high-value industries.

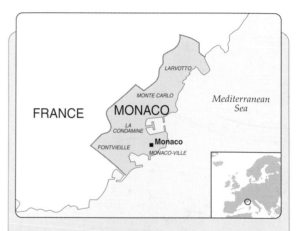

NATIONAL DATA – MONACO

Land area 1.95 sq km (0.75 sq mi)

Climate		Temperatures		Annual
	Altitude m (ft)	January °C (°F)	July °C (°F)	precipitation mm (in)
Monaco	55 (180)	10 (50)	24 (75)	816 (32.1)

Major physical features Mont Agel 140m (459ft)

Population (2006 est.) 32,543

Form of government nonparty constitutional monarchy with two legislative houses

Armed forces no armed forces

Capital city Monaco (15,500)

Official language French

Ethnic composition French 47%; Monegasque 16%; Italian 16%; other 21%

Religious affiliations Roman Catholic 90%; others 10%

Currency 1 euro (EUR) = 100 euro cents

Gross domestic product (2000) U.S. $870 million

Gross domestic product per capita (2000) U.S. $27,000

Life expectancy at birth male 75.85 yr; female 83.74 yr

Major resources tourism, financial services, property revenue, ceramics, metal works, textiles, instruments, plastics

FRANCE

NATIONAL DATA – FRANCE

Land area   545,630 sq km (210,669 sq mi)

Climate	Altitude m (ft)	Temperatures January °C (°F)	July °C (°F)	Annual precipitation mm (in)
Brest	103 (338)	7 (45)	17 (63)	1,145 (45)
Paris	53 (174)	5 (41)	20 (68)	650 (25.5)
Marseille	8 (26)	7 (45)	24 (75)	555 (21.8)

Major physical features   highest point: Mont Blanc 4,807 m (15,771 ft); longest river: Loire 1,020 km (634 mi)

Population   (2006 est.) 60,876,136

Form of government   multiparty republic with two legislative houses

Armed forces   army 137,000; navy 44,300; air force 64,000

Largest cities   Paris (capital – 2,142,800); Marseille (795,600); Lyon (468,300); Toulouse (426,700); Nice (339,000); Nantes (276,200); Strasbourg (273,100); Montpellier (244,700); Bordeaux (229,500); Lille (222,400)

Official language   French

Ethnic composition   French 90.6% (including Occitan 2.7%; Alsatian 2.3%; Breton 1%; Catalan 0.4%); Algerian 1.5%; Portuguese 1.4%; Moroccan 0.8%; Spanish 0.6%; Italian 0.6%; others 4.5%

Religious affiliations   Roman Catholic 83%–88%; Protestant 2%; Jewish 1%; Muslim 5%–10%; unaffiliated 4%

Currency   1 euro (EUR) = 100 euro cents

Gross domestic product   (2006) U.S. $1.871 trillion

Gross domestic product per capita   (2006) U.S. $30,100

Life expectancy at birth   male 76.1 yr; female 83.54 yr

Major resources   coal, iron ore, bauxite, zinc, uranium, antimony, arsenic, potash, feldspar, fluorospar, gypsum, timber, fish, barley, cattle, fruit, vegetables, grapes/wine, maize, oats, oil, natural gas, pigs, potatoes, poultry, salt, sheep, sugar beet, timber, uranium, wheat, tourism

France is the largest country in western Europe. Its varied landscapes include rolling plains, stunning river valleys, rocky and sandy beaches, remnants of ancient volcanoes and dramatic mountain scenery.

Geography

The Pyrenees mountains separate France from Spain, while the Alps form a barrier along the Italian border. In the interior the mountains of the Massif Central stretch to the sea; here on the Côte d'Azur lie the wealthy resort towns of the French Riviera. The north has a cool temperate climate, while the south has a Mediterranean climate of hot summers and mild, moist winters. Western regions are moderated by the Atlantic, but farther east the climate becomes more continental.

The fertile plains of the north and west rise to hills clad in gorse and heather, with oak growing in sheltered areas. There are lush pastures on the western and central slopes of the Pyrenees and Massif Central. In the southeast the vegetation is Mediterranean. Unique

The 16th-century Chambord Chateau in the Loire Valley, part of France's rich cultural heritage. It was a retreat for French kings, especially Louis XIV.

wildlife includes feral horses, bulls and flamingoes in the Camargue on the Rhône delta on the southern coast.

Society

France has a long history of cultural influence. Works by its painters, sculptors, writers, fashion designers, composers and film directors have enriched the world. France has also contributed significantly to international cuisine. The country became a republic in 1789 after ousting the Bourbon monarchy. In 1804 France expanded its empire under Napoleon Bonaparte. Following defeat by Germany in World War II, France's prosperity and pride were rebuilt by General de Gaulle, who also helped found what is now the EU.

Economy

France is the largest agricultural producer in western Europe and has benefited greatly from EU subsidies. Cereals, sugar beet and potatoes are the chief crops. Fruit is widely grown, especially in Brittany, Normandy, Aquitaine and the Rhône valley. France is also one of the world's largest wine producers and the third largest producer of raw timber.

The government has encouraged a shift to meat production, and so livestock is increasingly being reared. Fishing is confined mainly to the Atlantic coast.

Industry recovered after World War II thanks to U.S. aid from the Marshall Plan. France is now the world's fifth largest industrial power. There are few large companies, however, and most investment comes from the state. France is a leading steel, aircraft and automobile manufacturer. Other major industries are textiles, fuel refining, chemicals, perfume, fashion and tourism. France has a developed and comprehensive transport system, especially its rail network. The country's mineral resources are limited, and three-quarters of electrical power comes from state-owned nuclear plants.

FRANCE'S UNIQUE CHAMPAGNE

Of all wines none is so famous, or more copied, than champagne, a unique effervescent white wine. It comes from the region of chalky soils around Rheims, where summers are hot and winters are cold. No other region may legally call its wine champagne. The *méthode champenoise* – the process that adds the sparkle to the world-famous wine – is ascribed to Dom Pierre Pérignon, a cellarer and Benedictine monk, in the 17th century. Champagne making is a difficult and skillful process that can take several years. Vintage champagnes only come from wines produced in a particularly good year.

Map labels: Nord-Pas-de-Calais, Upper Normandy, Picardy, Alsace, Lower Normandy, Brittany, Île-de-France, Lorraine, Champagne-Ardenne, Pays de la Loire, Centre, Burgundy, Franche-Comté, Poitou-Charentes, Limousin, Rhône-Alpes, Aquitaine, Auvergne, Midi-Pyrénées, Provence-Alpes-Côte D'Azur, Languedoc-Roussillon, Corsica

BELGIUM

Belgium lies on the North Sea coast of Europe. Together with two of its neighbours, the Netherlands and Luxembourg, it is part of the Low Countries. Belgium belongs to NATO and is an important member of the EU, the main headquarters of which are in Brussels, the country's capital. Belgium's history has been closely linked to its bordering countries, and in the past it has suffered from having Germany and France as its nearest large neighbours. During World War I some of the bloodiest battles were fought on Belgian soil in places such as Passchendaele and Ypres.

Geography

Belgium's landscape divides naturally along the central valley of the Meuse River, with lowlands to the north and uplands to the south. The Belgian coastline has long sandy beaches bordered by dunes that broaden towards the French border. Behind the dunes a flat strip of polder land has been drained to create the characteristic landscape of dykes and canals. In the northeast

NATIONAL DATA – BELGIUM

Land area	30,278 sq km (11,690 sq mi)			

Climate		Temperatures		Annual
	Altitude m (ft)	January °C (°F)	July °C (°F)	precipitation mm (in)
Brussels	55 (180)	3 (37)	18 (64)	822 (32.3)

Major physical features   highest point: Botrange 694 m (2,276 ft); longest rivers: Meuse (part) 933 km (580 mi) and Schelde 432 km (270 mi)

Population   (2006 est.) 10,379,067

Form of government   multiparty federal monarchy with two legislative houses

Armed forces   army 24,800; navy 2,450; air force 10,240

Largest cities   Brussels (capital – 1,031,925); Antwerp (463,256); Gent (233,111); Charleroi (199,898); Liege (181,715); Brugge (116,618); Namur (106,539)

Official language   Dutch, French, German

Ethnic composition   Fleming 58%; Walloon 31%; mixed or other 11%

Religious affiliations   Roman Catholic 81%; Protestant or other Christian 7.3%; Muslim 3.6%; other 0.6%; nonreligious 7.5%

Currency   1 euro (EUR) = 100 euro cents

Gross domestic product   (2006) U.S. $330 billion

Gross domestic product per capita   (2005) U.S. $31,800

Life expectancy at birth   male 75.59 yr; female 82.09 yr

Major resources   construction materials, silica sand, carbonates, barley, coal, flax, hay, livestock, oats, potatoes, sugar beet, timber, vegetables, wheat, textiles, oil refining, diamond processing

the land rises to form heath and conifer forests. To the west, central Belgium forms a fertile plateau. Farther south is the high plateau of the Ardennes, whose mountains are cut by the deep wooded valleys of the Meuse and its tributaries. Near the German border is the Botrange, the highest point in Belgium. The extreme south is hilly and partly wooded.

Belgium has a temperate climate with plenty of rain. Half the land has been cleared for agriculture or pasture, but a reserve in the peat bogs of Haute Fagnes supports animals such as wild boar, wildcats, red deer and birds including owls and woodpeckers.

Society

The Low Countries, including Belgium, have been variously under the control of Romans, Franks, the Spanish and the French. Following the defeat of Napoleon in 1814, Belgium was united with the Netherlands, but it proclaimed national independence in 1831. In 1885 King Leopold II acquired the Congo in Africa, which became the Belgian Congo in 1908. As a result of the growing Flemish national movement, Belgium was divided in 1930 into French-speaking and Dutch-speaking areas. Belgium was invaded by Germany again in World War II.

Notable Belgians who have contributed to the arts include painter Pieter Breughel the Elder (c.1525–69) and composer César Franck (1822–90).

Economy

Belgium is an important centre of industry and commerce, and its economy is highly diversified. Its main

Canalside houses like this have given Brugge the name 'the Venice of the North'. The medieval city is the capital of the province of West Flanders.

trading partners are other EU member states. Farming concentrates on livestock production, with much of the arable land used for pasture and forage crops. Less than 3 percent of the labour force is employed on the land, and agriculture makes up only a tiny proportion of the country's income. About one-fifth of Belgium is forested, and the lumber industry has grown rapidly. Belgium has a small fleet of trawlers operating in the North Sea, and the catch – mostly herring and flatfish – meets about one-third of local demand.

Manufacturing accounts for nearly half the total value of Belgium's exports, although most raw materials are imported. Heavy industry is concentrated around the former coalfields of the Sambre-Meuse valley and north of Ghent. This includes glassmaking, metal refining and manufacture of heavy machinery. Arms manufacture is still important. Belgium produces rare metals such as cobalt and radium. Imported petroleum from the North Sea, the Middle East and the former Soviet Union is refined at Antwerp, and some is used for making plastics. Antwerp has been a diamond-cutting centre for more than 500 years and carries out 70 percent of the world's diamond dealing. Linen, wool, cotton and lace making are important industries, and Belgian chocolates are renowned worldwide. Banking, commerce and administration employ increasing numbers, and Belgium has benefited from being home to the headquarters of the European Commission, the Council of Ministers and the European Parliament.

ONE NATION, TWO LANGUAGES

More than half the population are Flemings; they live mostly in the north and speak Flemish, a highly localised version of Dutch. The French-speaking Walloons in the southern and eastern provinces make up the rest. However, a small number of German speakers live in the sparsely populated eastern districts (the Cantons de l'Est) of Liège province. Economic problems since the 1970s have mirrored Belgium's linguistic divide: high unemployment has arisen mainly in the Walloon south, while industry in the Flemish-speaking north has prospered.

NETHERLANDS

The small, densely populated Netherlands has a predominantly flat landscape, one-third of which lies below sea level. Moreover, vast tracts of land have been reclaimed from the sea. The Netherlands controls access to the sea from three major European rivers – the Schelde, the Meuse and the Rhine – making the country an important international commercial centre.

NATIONAL DATA – NETHERLANDS

Land area 33,883 sq km (13,082 sq mi)

Climate		Temperatures		Annual
	Altitude m (ft)	January °C (°F)	July °C (°F)	precipitation mm (in)
Amsterdam	–4 (–13)	3 (37)	17 (63)	831 (33)

Major physical features highest point: Vaalserberg (in far southeast) 321 m (1,053 ft); lowest point: (in the west) –7 m (–22 ft); longest rivers: Rhine (part) 1,319 km (820 mi) and Meuse (part) 933 km (580 mi)

Population (2006 est.) 16,491,461

Form of government multiparty constitutional monarchy with two legislative houses

Armed forces army 23,150; navy 12,130; air force 11,050

Largest cities Amsterdam (capital – 1,002,868); Rotterdam (989,956); The Hague (610,245); Utrecht (366,186); Eindhoven (302,274)

Official language Dutch

Ethnic composition Dutch 83%; other 17% (mainly Germans, Turks, Moroccans, Antilleans, Surinamese and Indonesians)

Religious affiliations Roman Catholic 31%; Dutch Reformed 13%; Calvinist 7%; Muslim 5.5%; other 2.5%; none 41%

Currency 1 euro (EUR) = 100 euro cents

Gross domestic product (2006) U.S. $512 billion

Gross domestic product per capita (2006) U.S. $31,7000

Life expectancy at birth male 76.39 yr; female 81.67 yr

Major resources natural gas, petroleum, peat, limestone, salt, sand, gravel, arable land, cereals, fish, fruit, vegetables, livestock, potatoes, poultry, sugar beet, horticultural plants

Geography

The north coast of the Netherlands is fringed by the long arc of the West Frisian Islands. They are formed from sandbars and dunes at the outer limits of the Wadden Zee. The Wadden Zee is separated from the freshwater Ijsselmeer by a 32-km (20-mi) dyke, which was part of a scheme to reclaim land from what was then the Zuider Zee. While the dyke was under construction, the Wieringermeer to the southwest was drained. This became the first of four polders to be reclaimed, and today they cover more than 2,000 sq km (800 sq mi). The provinces of North and South Holland are older reclaimed lands. In southwestern Zeeland, the rivers Schelde, Meuse and Rhine flow into the North Sea via a delta. Inland, flat clay lowlands of the north give way to sandy soils elsewhere. In the southernmost

province of Limburg, a chalk plateau rises towards Vaalserberg, the highest point of the Netherlands. Summers are relatively cool, and winters are usually mild and wet. Rainfall is frequent throughout the year.

The vegetation is a mixture of planted oak, birch and coniferous woodlands, with scrubland behind the protective coastal dunes. The Wadden Zee, with its mudflats, marshes and dunes, is Europe's most important wetland habitat.

Society

The history of the Netherlands is intimately connected with the other Low Countries, Belgium and Luxembourg, and many attempts have been made to unite them all. The Dutch have a strong trading tradition, and set up the Dutch East India Company in the 15th century to exploit the spice trade. The Netherlands were occupied by Germany in World War II. After the war American economic aid, part of the Marshall Plan, helped the Dutch create a powerful industrial base, and neutrality was abandoned in favor of full participation in western European affairs. The country is a member of NATO and of the EU. The Netherlands has a large immigrant community, including people from former Dutch colonies. A strong cultural tradition, particularly in music and art, is exemplified by the painter Vincent Van Gogh (1853–90).

Windmills have been used since the 15th century to help drain the flat, low-lying marshlands for farming.

GETTING RID OF THE WATER

Because the Netherlands are flat and very low-lying, it is necessary to drain the land before it can be used for agriculture or other purposes, and to reduce the risk of flooding. As early as 1000 A.D. simple sluices were in use to improve drainage. Four hundred years later the clay flats of the west and north were criss-crossed with an intricate network of dykes and drains. From the 15th to the 17th centuries windmills were built on a large scale to pump water from the low-lying land behind the dykes, creating polders – areas where the water can be controlled – for farming. Steam pumps were introduced in the 19th century, making it possible to reclaim the Haarlemmermeer Polder in 1852.

Economy

About one-fifth of the land is agricultural, and two-thirds of this is pasture. Farms are large and highly mechanised, but employ only a small percentage of the workforce. The country is a major exporter of farm produce, and these commodities account for nearly one-quarter of all exports. Crop farming is less important, but the bulb and cut-flower industry is large, and exports go all over the world. Fishing is small-scale and concentrates on shellfish.

During the 1950s substantial oil and gas reserves were discovered. Much of the gas is exported. The Netherlands produces its own crude petroleum from wells in Drenthe and South Holland. There is also a large storage, refining and petrochemical complex at Europoort outside Rotterdam. Elsewhere, smelting plants fuelled by natural gas extract aluminum. About one-seventh of the labor force works in manufacturing, chiefly in food processing, chemicals and petrochemicals, vehicles, computers and electronics. Exports from the Netherlands amount to half the country's income. More than half of all external trade is with Belgium, Luxembourg and Germany. Road, canal and rail systems are extensive to cope with the haulage, and Rotterdam-Europoort, the largest port in Europe, handles the biggest tonnage of any harbour in the world.

NATIONAL DATA – GERMANY

Land area 349,223 sq km (89,166 sq mi)

Climate	Altitude m (ft)	Temperatures January °C (°F)	July °C (°F)	Annual precipitation mm (in)
Berlin	55 (180)	-1 (30)	19 (66)	580 (23)
Hamburg	14 (46)	1 (34)	17 (63)	772 (30.3)
Munich	528 (1,732)	-2 (29)	17 (63)	928 (37)

Major physical features highest point: Zugspitze 2,963 m (9,720 ft); longest rivers: Danube (part) 2,850 km (1,771 mi), Rhine (part) 1,319 km (820 mi); Elbe (part) 1,165 km (724 mi); largest lake: Lake Constance (part) 544 sq km (210 sq mi)

Population (2006 est.) 82,422,299

Form of government multiparty republic with two legislative houses

Armed forces army 191,500; navy 25,600; air force 67,500

Largest cities Berlin (capital – 3,388,477); Hamburg (1,734,083); Munich (1,247,873); Cologne (965,954); Frankfurt (643,432); Dortmund (589,661); Essen (589,499); Stuttgart (589,161); Düsseldorf (572,511); Bremen (544,853)

Official language German

Ethnic composition German 88.2%; Turkish 3.4%; other 8.4% (mainly Greek, Italian, Polish, Russian, Serbo-Croatian, Spanish)

Religious affiliations Protestant 34%; Roman Catholic 34%; Muslim 3.7%; unaffiliated or other 28.3%

Currency 1 euro (EUR) = 100 euro cents

Gross domestic product (2006) U.S. $2.585 trillion

Gross domestic product per capita (2005) U.S. $31,400

Life expectancy at birth male 75.81 yr; female 81.96 yr

Major resources coal, lignite, natural gas, iron ore, copper, nickel, uranium, potash, salt, construction materials, timber, antimony, arsenic, barley, bismuth, cobalt, fish, fruit, vegetables, grapes/wine, beer, lead, livestock, dairy products, oats, potatoes, rye, sugar beet, wheat, zinc, tourism

Germany is Europe's second most populous country, with nine other European countries at its borders.

Geography

Germany's varied landscapes reflect western, central and eastern Europe. The North German Plain is part of a lowland belt stretching from France to Russia. The central uplands is a mountainous arc that sweeps across Europe from France to the Carpathians. Farther south, the main river valleys divide the upland belt into ranges. In the centre of Germany are two huge volcanic plateaus, the Vogelsberg and the Rhön. Much of central-southern Germany is a low plateau with river valleys. In the southwest the Black Forest peaks look across to their French counterparts, the Vosges. Germany's most dramatic scenery is in the far south, where the Bavarian plateau rises towards the northern Alps. The Zugspitze is found here. Germany's Baltic coast has low cliffs and sandy beaches. The North Sea coast has dykes

underdeveloped, with outdated, polluting industries. Addressing these problems is stretching the country's resources. Agriculture is second to industry in terms of economic importance, although brewing, wine making and dairy farming make significant contributions. A large fishing fleet operates in many waters. Mining and manufacturing account for one-quarter of the nation's income. Most energy comes from burning fossil fuels, but there are 21 nuclear and hydroelectric plants. Manufactured goods include chemicals, machinery, automobiles, textiles and precision equipment.

The Brandenburg Gate, Berlin, at night. This triumphal arch, a symbol of Germany, is the only remaining one in a series of arches that once marked the entry points into the city.

protecting reclaimed farmland. The country's climate becomes more continental towards the south and east. Almost 30 percent of Germany is wooded.

Society

Germany's legacy of art and literature is exemplified by composers such as Ludwig van Beethoven (1770–1827) and Richard Wagner (1813–83). Today, ethnic Germans make up most of the population, but the country is also home to minorities such as Turks and Yugoslavs who came as 'guest workers' to postwar Germany. Since 1990 the country has taken in many refugees from Africa, Asia and Europe, stoking right-wing opposition.

Economy

Defeated in two world wars in the 20th century, West Germany recovered to become the wealthiest nation in Europe. Reunification in 1990, however, had a negative impact on the economy, because East Germany was

A REUNIFIED GERMANY

At the end of World War II Germany lost all territories east of the Oder and Neisse Rivers and was divided into occupation zones by Britain, France, the United States and the Soviet Union. In 1949 the British, French and U.S. zones were consolidated into the Federal Republic of West Germany. The Soviet Union created the communist German Democratic Republic (East Germany), and established a guarded cordon along the border in 1952. West Berlin became an isolated enclave 190 km (120 mi) inside East Germany, and a favoured destination for refugees. The 1980s saw pressure for reform in the Soviet bloc, and in 1989 the border between East and West Germany was opened. East Germany's communist government collapsed in 1990, and later that year East and West Germany reunited.

SWITZERLAND

The most mountainous country in Europe, landlocked Switzerland is a federal state made up of 26 separate cantons, with four different languages. Yet the Swiss nation preserves a high degree of unity. Mountains dominate the landscape, with the Alps occupying three-fifths of the country. The highest peaks are in the Pennine Alps in the southwest, along the Italian border. There also spectacular lakes, such as Lake Lucerne, Lake Lugarno and Lake Geneva. The climate is temperate continental. Lower slopes support woodland, while the alpine regions are home to chamois, ibex and the rare edelweiss flower.

Switzerland is one of the world's most prosperous countries. Its geographical location, tradition of confidentiality, and political stability have made it a centre for international finance. There is little flat farmland, but Swiss cheese and chocolate are exported worldwide. Hydroelectric power supplies most of the country's needs, with nuclear power providing the rest. High-grade manufactured goods including chemicals and precision instruments form the mainstay of the economy. Trade tariffs provide the greater part of federal government revenue, while tourism is an all-year-around source of income. Foreigners, especially Italians and Croats, provide unskilled, low-paid labour.

A typical Swiss mountain scene in summer, showing a green landscape dotted with wooden chalets. In midwinter, temperatures normally fall below freezing everywhere, and the highest Alps lie beneath perpetual snow.

NATIONAL DATA – SWITZERLAND

Land area 39,770 sq km (15,355 sq mi)

Climate	Altitude m (ft)	Temperatures January °C (°F)	July °C (°F)	Annual precipitation mm (in)
Zurich	540 (1,772)	0 (32)	18 (79)	1,086 (42.7)

Major physical features highest point: Monte Rosa 3,505 m (11,500 ft); longest river: Rhine (part) 1,319 km (820 mi), Rhone (part) 813 km (505 mi); largest lake: Lake Constance (part) 544 sq km (210 sq mi)

Population (2006 est.) 7,523,934

Form of government federal multiparty republic with two legislative houses

Armed forces joint forces 4,300

Largest cities Zurich (342,518); Geneva (177,535); Basel (165,051); Bern (capital – 122,707); Lausanne (116,332); Lucerne (116,332)

Official language German, French, Italian, Romansch

Ethnic composition German 65%; French 18%; Italian 10%; Romansch 1%; other 6%

Religious affiliations Roman Catholic 41.8%; Protestant 35.3%; Orthodox 1.8%; other Christian 0.4%; Muslim 4.3%; other 1%; unspecified 4.3%; none 11.1%

Currency 1 Swiss franc (CHF) = 100 centimes

Gross domestic product (2005) U.S. $241.8 billion

Gross domestic product per capita (2005) U.S. $32,300

Life expectancy at birth male 77.69 yr; female 83.48 yr

Major resources hydropower, timber, salt, apples, barley, building stone, grapes, livestock, potatoes, salt, wheat, tourism

AUSTRIA

Landlocked Austria lies at the crossroads of western and eastern Europe, ensuring its influence on the continent's political and economic life. The magnificent alpine scenery, together with the cosmopolitan atmosphere and cultural attractions of its cities, also make it a great centre of tourism. The Alps cover nearly two-thirds of the country, stretching from west to east. There are lowlands to the east, and hill country along the borders with the Czech Republic and Slovakia.

NATIONAL DATA - AUSTRIA

Land area 82,444 sq km (31,832 sq mi)

Climate	Altitude m (ft)	Temperatures January °C (°F)	July °C (°F)	Annual precipitation mm (in)
Vienna	212 (695)	−3 (27)	20 (68)	620 (24.4)

Major physical features highest point: Grossglockner 3,801 m (12,470 ft); longest rivers: Danube (part) 2,850 km (1,770 mi), Inn (part) 510 km (317 mi)

Population (2006 est.) 8,192,880

Form of government federal multiparty republic with two legislative houses

Armed forces army 33,200; air force 6,700

Largest cities Vienna (capital - 1,651,365); Graz (244,537); Linz (188,407); Salzburg (148,549); Innsbruck (116,881)

Official language German

Ethnic composition Austrians 91.1%; former Yugoslavs 4% (includes Croatians, Slovenes, Serbs and Bosniaks); Turks 1.6%; German 0.9%; other or unspecified 2.4%

Religious affiliations Roman Catholic 73.6%; Protestant 4.7%; Muslim 4.2%; other 3.5%; unspecified 2%; none 12%

Currency 1 euro (EUR) = 100 euro cents

Gross domestic product (2006) U.S. $279.5 billion

Gross domestic product per capita (2006) U.S. $34,100

Life expectancy at birth male 76.17 yr; female 82.11 yr

Major resources oil, coal, lignite, timber, iron ore, copper, zinc, antimony, magnesite, tungsten, graphite, salt, hydropower, anhydrous gypsum, barley, cattle, clay, hay, fodder, kaolin, maize (corn), natural gas, potatoes, sheep, sugar beet, talc, temperate fruits, vines/wine, wheat, tourism

Austria was once one of the greatest empires in the history of Europe, a fact reflected in the grand architecture of many of its imposing buildings.

The southern and western mountains have an alpine climate with plenty of rain; the northeast has a drier, more continental climate. Forests and meadows cover most of the landscape, and strict conservation laws protect the remaining ibex, chamois and rare birds. Only 20 percent of land is arable, but intensive farming practices mean the country is 75 percent self-sufficient in cereals and vegetables. There is a flourishing wine industry. Austria is rich in mineral and energy resources, and mining and energy production are nationalised. Austria is a leading oil producer, but hydroelectricity supplies most of the country's power. Metals, chemicals, plastics and electrical goods are manufactured.

LUXEMBOURG

LIECHTENSTEIN

The tiny landlocked state of Luxembourg is a constitutional monarchy. Despite the strong influence of its larger neighbours, Luxembourg has a strong sense of identity and has kept its own language – Letzeburgesch – alongside French and German. Two-thirds of the land (the central and southern regions) has beds of iron ore covered by fertile soil and woodland. The north is high plateau. Despite being strongly agricultural, Luxembourg's prosperity depends almost entirely on heavy industry and international finance. Favourable tax laws encourage companies to register there, and Luxembourg boasts more than 200 different banks.

Although Liechtenstein belongs to the Swiss customs union and uses Swiss currency, it is nevertheless an independent state. To the north and west the land is a broad floodplain bordering the Rhine; to the east the foothills of the Alps rise to snow-capped peaks. About two-fifths of the land is forest, and alpine plants grow above the treeline. In 1930 most Liechtensteiners were farmers; now less than one in 40 of the population works on the land. There are no raw materials, and manufacturing concentrates on small-scale items such as optical equipment. The economy depends on revenue earned through the banking sector and tourism.

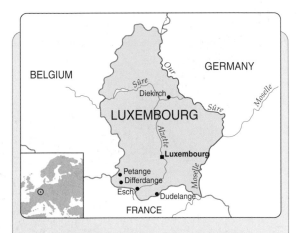

NATIONAL DATA – LUXEMBOURG

Land area 2,586 sq km (998 sq mi)

Climate		Temperatures		Annual
	Altitude m (ft)	January °C (°F)	July °C (°F)	precipitation mm (in)
Luxembourg	330 (1,082)	0 (32)	17 (63)	874 (34.4)

Major physical features highest point: Wemperhardt 559 m (1,843 ft); longest river: Moselle (part) 545 km (340 mi)

Population (2006 est.) 474,413

Form of government multiparty constitutional monarchy with one legislative house

Armed forces army 900

Capital city Luxembourg (76,420)

Official language French, German, Letzeburgesch

Ethnic composition Luxembourger 72.5%; Portuguese 9%; Italian 5.4%; French 3.4%; Belgian 2.5%; German 2.4%; others 4.8%

Religious affiliations 87% Roman Catholic; Protestants, Jews and Muslims 13%

Currency 1 euro (EUR) = 100 euro cents

Gross domestic product (2006) U.S. $32.6 billion

Gross domestic product per capita (2006) U.S. $68,800

Life expectancy at birth male 75.6 yr; female 82.38 yr

Major resources iron ore (no longer exploited), cattle, cereals, dairy, grapes, potatoes

NATIONAL DATA – LIECHTENSTEIN

Land area 160 sq km (62 sq mi)

Climate temperate continental

Major physical features highest point: Grauspitz 2,599 m (8,527 ft)

Population (2006 est.) 33,987

Form of government Hereditary constitutional monarchy on a democratic and parliamentary basis

Capital city Vaduz (5,038)

Official language German

Ethnic composition Alemannic 86%; Italian, Turkish and other 14%

Religious affiliations Roman Catholic 76.2%; Protestant 7%; unknown 10.6%; other 6.2%

Currency 1 Swiss franc (CHF) = 100 centimes

Gross domestic product (2001) U.S. $1.786 billion

Gross domestic product per capita (1999) U.S. $25,000

Life expectancy at birth male 76.1 yr; female 83.28 yr

Major resources hydroelectric potential, grapes, livestock, maize (corn), potatoes, timber, vegetables, wheat, tourism

SLOVAKIA

Until 1993 part of the former Czechoslovakia, Slovakia is a newly created state at the centre of Europe. Separation from the Czech Republic gave Slovakia complete independence for the first time in 1,000 years. The country is mostly mountainous, with lowland plains around the Danube basin on the southern and eastern borders. To the west, the Carpathian Mountains rise steeply from the border with the Czech Republic. The climate is continental, with cold winters and warm summers, often with thunderstorms.

Only one-third of Slovakia's land is cultivated. Major crops include wheat, sugar beet, barley and potatoes. Sheep, pigs and cattle are the main livestock animals. Forestry is also important. Iron, copper, lead, manganese and zinc are mined from various locations but not in large quantities. Coal is used mainly for energy generation, although the chief source of power is hydroelectricity. The biggest sector of the economy is still manufacturing. It remains manpower-heavy, however, employing 29 percent of the workforce. Extensive reforms and privatisation have taken place within the industrial and financial sectors.

Typical Slovak mountain scenery – villages nestling on rolling countryside, with coniferous forest cladding the foothills. The extensive forests supply the country's lumber and paper industries.

NATIONAL DATA - SLOVAKIA

Land area	48,800 sq km (18,842 sq mi)			

Climate		Temperatures		Annual
	Altitude m (ft)	January °C (°F)	July °C (°F)	precipitation mm (in)
Bratislava	132 (433)	–1 (30)	21 (70)	557 (21.9)

Major physical features   highest point: Gerlach Peak 2,655 m (8,711 ft); longest rivers: Danube (part) 2,850 km (1,771 mi), Vah 394 km (245 mi)

Population   (2006 est.) 5,439,448

Form of government   multiparty parliamentary democracy with one legislative house

Armed forces   army 12,860; navy 5,160; joint forces 2,175

Largest cities   Bratislava (capital – 425,533); Kosice (235,281); Presov (92,147); Zilina (85,278); Nitra (86,138)

Official language   Slovak

Ethnic composition   Slovak 85.8%; Hungarian 9.7%; Roma 1.7%; Ruthenian/Ukrainian 1%; other and unspecified 1.8%

Religious affiliations   Roman Catholic 68.9%; Protestant 10.8%; Greek Catholic 4.1%; other or unspecified 3.2%; none 13%

Currency   1 Slovak koruna (SKK) = 100 hellers

Gross domestic product   (2006) U.S. $96.35 billion

Gross domestic product per capita   (2006) U.S. $17,700

Life expectancy at birth   male 70.76 yr; female 78.89 yr

Major resources   brown coal and lignite; small amounts of iron ore, copper, manganese ore, zinc, salt, antimony, cereals, livestock, magnesium, mercury, potatoes, sugar beet, barley, timber, uranium

CZECH REPUBLIC

In 1993 the former eastern bloc state of Czechoslovakia split into two new republics: the Czech Republic and Slovakia. Most of the Czech Republic occupies the territory of the ancient Kingdom of Bohemia; Moravia and parts of Silesia (the rest of which is modern Poland) make up the remainder of this state, located in the heart of central Europe.

NATIONAL DATA – CZECH REPUBLIC

Land area 77,276 sq km (29,836 sq mi)

Climate	Altitude m (ft)	Temperatures January °C (°F)	July °C (°F)	Annual precipitation mm (in)
Prague	374 (1,227)	-3 (27)	18 (64)	526 (20.7)

Major physical features highest point: Mt Snezka (Sudetic Mountains) 1,602 m (5,256 ft); longest rivers: Elbe (part) 1,165 km (724 mi), Vltava 430 km (267 mi)

Population (2006 est.) 10,235,455

Form of government multiparty parliamentary democracy with two legislative houses

Armed forces army 16,663; air force 5,609

Largest cities Prague (capital – 1,181,610); Brno (366,757); Ostrava (310,078); Plzen (162,759)

Official language Czech

Ethnic composition Czech 90.4%; Moravian 3.7%; Slovak 1.9%; other 4%

Religious affiliations Roman Catholic 26.8%; Protestant 2.1%; other 3.3%; unspecified 8.8%; unaffiliated 59%

Currency 1 Czech koruna (CZK) = 100 halura

Gross domestic product (2006) U.S. $221.4 billion

Gross domestic product per capita (2006) U.S. $21,600

Life expectancy at birth male 72.94 yr; female 79.69 yr

Major resources hard coal, lignite, kaolin, clay, graphite, timber, antimony, cereals, iron ore, livestock, magnesium, mercury, potatoes, sugar beet, uranium, beer, tourism

Geography

In the west the Bohemian massif and plateau occupy the greater part of the former Kingdom of Bohemia. This high, broken plateau is encircled by a number of mountain chains: the Ore Mountains, the Bohemian Forest, the Sudetic Mountains and the Bohemian-Moravian Heights. The Carpathian Mountains separate the Czech Republic from Slovakia. The central plateau is crossed by the Elbe and Vltava Rivers, which merge near Prague. Southeast of the Bohemian-Moravian Heights lies the Morava River valley in the heart of Moravia; here hills and valleys surround the ancient Moravian capital of Brno. The Czech Republic lies in the middle of a climatic transition zone. To the west of the country the climate is mostly maritime, but to the east it is increasingly continental. Precipitation is generally low on the Bohemian plateau and in the plains, both of which are sheltered by the mountains of Slovakia from winds bringing rain and snow.

The old town square in Prague. The capital is also now a major tourist destination, full of bars, restaurants and historic sights.

and in southern Moravia. Pigs, cattle and poultry are the chief livestock animals.

Minerals are limited, the most important being coking coal. Poor-quality brown coal (lignite) is mined, mainly for power generation, but its use is controversial, since it causes heavy industrial pollution. Most oil and gas are imported. Abundant coal and iron ore have made iron and steelworking the major industries in the Czech Republic. Other important sectors included heavy machinery, Bohemian glass and Pilsner beer.

Until 1990 trade was mainly with the Soviet Union, and Czech goods were barely competitive in world markets. In the early 1990s an increasing budget deficit, almost 10 percent of GDP in 1996, led to investment failures and a currency crisis. As a result, the government introduced austerity packages and a revitalisation program aimed at attracting foreign investment and privatising state enterprises. The Czech Republic has attracted considerable foreign investment – over 80 percent of it German – and its economy is increasingly linked to that of Germany. In fact, Germany is the republic's largest trading partner, taking 40 percent of exports and providing 27 percent of imports. Tourism to Prague has become an important foreign currency earner. The country became a member of the EU in 1994.

Society

The former republic of Czechoslovakia was created in 1918, after the collapse of the Austro-Hungarian empire in World War I. Tomáš Masaryk (1850–1937) became its first president. The country was invaded by Germany during World War II, and the communists seized power in 1948. The 'people's republic' was changed to the 'socialistic republic' in 1960. The republic lasted until 1 January 1993, when Czechoslovakia split to form two new, fully independent countries.

Economy

With the advent of communism in the 1950s, agriculture was collectivised. Since then, industry has encroached heavily on farmland, and the country is no longer self-sufficient in food. Major crops include wheat, barley, sugar beet and potatoes, but yields are decreasing. Hops are grown around Plzen, home of Pilsner beers. There are vineyards along the Vltava River

EVENTS OF THE 'PRAGUE SPRING'

After World War II the former state of Czechoslovakia was more or less a Soviet satellite. But in the 1960s pressures began to build for economic and political reforms, and in 1967 the hardline president Antonin Novotny was replaced by Alexander Dubček. The period of political tolerance and reform that followed became known as the 'Prague Spring'. Alarmed that the Czech example might be copied by other eastern European satellite states, the Soviet Union invaded Czechoslovakia under the pretext of 'defending socialism', put down the resistance, and installed a puppet government.

POLAND

The east-central European state of Poland is surrounded by seven other nations. The country is for the most part low-lying, the only mountainous areas being the Sudetic Mountains in the southwest and the Tatra and Carpathian Mountains in the far south along the border with Slovakia. Formerly a Soviet satellite, Poland was in 1989 one of the first of several European countries to break free of the communist system.

NATIONAL DATA – POLAND

Land area	304,465 sq km (117,555 sq mi)

Climate	Altitude m (ft)	Temperatures January °C (°F)	July °C (°F)	Annual precipitation mm (in)
Gdansk	12 (39)	-2 (28)	17 (63)	497 (19.5)
Warsaw	110 (361)	-2 (28)	18 (64)	520 (20.4)

Major physical features highest point: Rysy (Tatra Mountains) 2,498 m (8,197 ft); lowest point: near Gulf of Gdansk -10 m (-33 ft); longest river: Vistula 1,086 km (675 mi)

Population (2006 est.) 38,536,869

Form of government multiparty republic with two legislative houses

Armed forces army 89,000; navy 14,300; air force 30,000

Largest cities Warsaw (capital – 1,692,854); Lodz (774,004); Krakow (757,430); Wroclaw (636,268); Poznan (570,828); Gdansk (459,072); Szczecin (411,900); Bydgoszcz (368,235); Lublin (355,998)

Official language Polish

Ethnic composition Polish 96.7%; German 0.4%; Belarusian 0.1%; Ukrainian 0.1%; other and unspecified 2.7%

Religious affiliations Roman Catholic 89.8% (75% practicing); Eastern Orthodox 1.3%; Protestant 0.3%; other 0.3%; unspecified 8.3%

Currency 1 zloty (PLN) = 100 groszy

Gross domestic product (2006) U.S. $542.6 billion

Gross domestic product per capita (2006) U.S. $14,100

Life expectancy at birth male 70.95 yr; female 79.23 yr

Major resources coal, sulphur, copper, natural gas, oil, silver, lead, salt, amber, cereals, fish, iron ore, livestock, oil seed, potatoes, sugar beet, timber, zinc

Geography

In the northwest the Baltic coast is fringed with sandy beaches and dunes. South of this region, but reaching the coast at Gdansk, is a range of hills enclosing a lake-strewn hinterland known as Pomerania. The central lowlands to the south, covering one-third of the country, are Poland's richest agricultural area. In the east the capital, Warsaw, lies on the banks of the Vistula, Poland's longest river. Uplands border the southern flank of the central plains. The two main areas here are the Lubin plateau and Little Poland. The latter includes two higher mountain ranges, the Jura and the thickly forested Holy Cross Mountains. Poland's highest mountains lie in the far south. Poland has few climatic contrasts. The south and east of the country have a continental climate, with cold winters and warm

summers. In the northwest summers are cooler and winters milder. To the south, in the mountains, winter snows may be heavy.

Once densely forested, much of Poland is now farmland. The Bialowieza National Park on the Belorussian border in the east is primeval forest, and has the last remaining European bison stocks.

History

Poland's turbulent history is long and complex. Tradition dates its foundation to 966 A.D. After the Russian Revolution of 1917, Poland's independence was recognised by the Bolsheviks. In 1939 Poland was invaded by Nazi Germany, triggering World War II. Devastated by war, and with its population greatly reduced – especially by the genocide against the country's Jews – Poland became a communist satellite. Protests against the communist regime were brutally suppressed. But a tide of dissent, fuelled by renewed hope after the election of a Polish pope in 1978 and the *Solidarnosc* (solidarity) shipyard strikes, led in 1989 to free-market reforms and later the election of noncommunist leaders.

Renowned Poles include astronomer Copernicus (1473–1543) and composer Frédéric Chopin (1810–49).

Wawel Cathedral in Krakow was the coronation place of Polish monarchs. Part of the nave is a mausoleum to St. Stanislav, patron saint of Poland.

Economy

In 1989 Poland began to transform itself from a one-party state into a parliamentary democracy, achieving the change in a very short space of time. Simultaneously, the country dismantled its centralised, state-controlled economy in favour of the free-market system. The major industries were privatised, subsidies were abolished, foreign investment was encouraged and exchange rates were set at commercial levels. By the late 1990s the economy was one of the fastest-growing for a former communist country. Now new skyscrapers rise above city skylines, and shops and cafes look like those in any modern society. Poland is now also a member of the EU.

Almost half of Poland's land area is given over to arable farming; the main crops are potatoes, sugar beet and cereals. Extensive pastureland supports pigs and cattle, and forestry produces timber for export. Rich coal reserves have provided Poland with a valuable export for years. Other minerals include sulphur, zinc and lead; in 1985 oil was discovered off the coast. Most of Poland's electricity comes from coal-fired power stations. The communist years emphasised engineering and heavy industry – much of it outdated and polluting – at the expense of consumer manufacturing, and adapting to a free-market economy has required extensive changes and continues to present great challenges.

COMMUNICATIONS

Poland has an extensive rail network, and many of the railways were electrified after World War II. The road network is also well developed, and it was once an important link between former Soviet bloc countries for freight transport. The main ports, situated at Szczecin, Gdynia and Gdansk, have busy international shipping schedules. The state airline, LOT, provides travel to international and internal destinations, and the country is also a popular destination for other airlines. Polish Radio and Television (PRT) has several radio and television channels, and also has satellite links with other networks throughout the world.

HUNGARY

One of the oldest states in eastern Europe, with an ancient Magyar culture, landlocked Hungary was one of several former Soviet satellites that found itself on the path towards democracy following the liberalisation of the economic and political structures of the country in the late 1980s. As in many other former eastern bloc countries, the transition to a successful free-market economy has not been easy to achieve, however.

NATIONAL DATA – HUNGARY

Land area	92,340 sq km (35,653 sq mi)			

Climate		Temperatures		Annual
	Altitude m (ft)	January °C (°F)	July °C (°F)	precipitation mm (in)
Budapest	139 (456)	-1 (30)	21 (70)	516 (20.3)

Major physical features highest point: Kékes 1,014 m (3,327 ft); longest river: Danube (part) 2,850 km (1,771 mi); largest lake: Lake Balaton 601 sq km (232 sq mi)

Population (2006 est.) 9,981,334

Form of government multiparty republic with one legislative house

Armed forces army 23,950; navy 7,500; joint forces 850

Largest cities Budapest (capital – 1,697,343); Debrecen (204,297); Miskolc (175,701); Szeged (162,889); Pécs (156,567)

Official language Hungarian

Ethnic composition Hungarian 92.3%; Roma 1.9%; other or unknown 5.8%

Religious affiliations Roman Catholic 51.9%; Calvinist 15.9%; Lutheran 3%; Greek Catholic 2.6%; other Christian 1%; other or unspecified 11.1%; unaffiliated 14.5%

Currency 1 forint (HUF) = 100 filler

Gross domestic product (2006) U.S. $172.7 billion

Gross domestic product per capita (2006) U.S. $17,300

Life expectancy at birth male 68.45 yr; female 77.14 yr

Major resources bauxite, lignite, natural gas, tourism, cereals, fruit, vegetables, grapes/wine, livestock, oil, potatoes, sugar beet, sunflowers

Geography

Hungary is mainly low-lying, with the broad, fertile plains of the central Danube basin extending across much of the country. Low hills and mountains dominate the north and west. A rich lowland area – the Great Hungarian Plain – extends eastwards from the Danube, which flows south across the centre of the country. West of the Danube lies hilly Transdanubia, rising to mountains. To the northwest is the Little Hungarian Plain, a lowland area bounded to the north by the Danube. Hungary has a continental climate, with cold winters and warm summers. Droughts are common in summer, and thawing snows on the mountains in neighbouring countries swell Hungary's rivers in spring.

The once-extensive forests were cleared long ago, but some small broad-leaf forests survive. Wild boar and deer are still abundant in reafforested mountain areas. The marshlands are a paradise for waterfowl such as flamingoes and spoonbills. Environmental damage has been caused by poorly controlled industrial pollution, and conservation programs have yet to make an impact.

Society

Hungary has been settled by many different peoples in its history, but native Hungarians – descendants of the Magyars, originally nomadic horsemen – maintain a strong national identity. Past rulers of Hungary include the empires of Bulgaria, Rome, the Mongols, the Turks and the Habsburgs. World War I shattered the Austro-Hungarian Empire: two-thirds of Hungary was annexed by surrounding countries, and the rest fell to a communist coup. During World War II Hungary sided with the Nazis, and as the Soviet army swept westwards in 1945, Hungary became subsumed within the eastern bloc until the late 1980s.

Economy

During the 1990s the former communist-controlled economy gave way to free-market capitalism, and by 2000 over 85 percent of the economy was privatised. Trade with the EU has greatly increased (Hungary joined the EU in 2004), with Germany, Austria and Italy among its major trading partners. About one-half of all foreign investment in Hungary has been in the capital, Budapest, which is now one of the largest shopping centres in the entire eastern European region.

As much as three-fifths of the country is rich arable land, and Hungary is virtually self-sufficient in food. Since 1990 land has been restored to precollectivisation owners. The main crops are cereals, sugar beet and sunflowers. Pigs and poultry make up the bulk of the farmed livestock. Vineyards, mainly in upland regions, yield some excellent wines, which are exported. Commercial forestry along the Tisza River supplies produce for the cellulose industry. Hungary's main mineral resources include low-grade coal (lignite), the chief fuel for generating energy. Only small deposits of natural gas and petroleum have been exploited.

Manufacturing industries are intensive, particularly around Budapest. Products include automobiles, engineering and chemicals. Lighter manufacturing has grown in importance. Tourism has expanded enormously, especially in Budapest. Hungary's road and rail networks are well developed but increasingly congested. The Danube carries a vast amount of freight by water, especially from abroad, and the national airline is a significant international carrier.

View of Pest on the east bank of the Danube River from Buda on the west bank. To the right is the famous linking Chain Bridge.

HUNGARY'S TURKISH LEGACY

Of the various powers that controlled Hungary throughout its history, one of the most influential was the Ottoman Empire, which annexed much of the country during the 16th century. The Turks set about converting churches into mosques and generally imposing their influence on architecture. Many Turkish buildings were destroyed by their successors, the Habsburgs, but the Turkish influence can still be seen in many artefacts. Among the best-known are the elaborately designed Turkish baths, for which Hungary is famous. In Budapest millions of gallons of mineralised water pour out from natural hot springs each day and are used in thermal pools, spas and public baths.

SLOVENIA

The first of the former Yugoslav republics to declare independence in 1991, Slovenia was formally recognised as a new state in 1992. Situated at the northern end of the Balkan Peninsula, most of the country is mountainous, except for the lowlands near the coast. The Alps extend into Slovenia from Italy and Austria, and from them the landscape descends through dense woodlands to fertile valleys. In the east, the Drava River flows through rich agricultural land. Western Slovenia has a Mediterranean climate, while the eastern part is more continental.

Before the breakup of Yugoslavia, Slovenia was the most prosperous of the constituent republics, generating 20 percent of the country's income. Civil war and sanctions damaged the economy, but it had largely recovered by the mid-1990s and was boosted by joining the EU. Agriculture is centred on rearing livestock, with substantial cereal, potato and sugar beet production. Wine production is also well established. Iron and steel are the major industries in Ljubljana, and textile factories are located throughout the country. Slovenia also has plentiful reserves of lignite, lead and mercury.

A rural view of Slovenia from the air, showing fields and villages with mountains in the distance.

NATIONAL DATA – SLOVENIA

Land area	20,151 sq km (7,780 sq mi)			

Climate		Temperatures		Annual
	Altitude m (ft)	January °C (°F)	July °C (°F)	precipitation mm (in)
Ljubljana	448 (1,469)	0 (32)	21 (70)	1,266 (49.8)

Major physical features   highest point: Triglav 2,864 m (9,396 ft); longest river: Sava (part) 940 km (584 mi)

Population   (2006 est.) 2,010,347

Form of government   multiparty republic with two legislative houses

Armed forces   army 6,550

Largest cities   Ljubljana (capital – 247,772); Maribor (91,540); Celje (36,369)

Official language   Slovene

Ethnic composition   Slovene 83.1%; Serb 2%; Croat 1.8%; Bosniak 1.1%; other or unspecified 12%

Religious affiliations   Catholic 57.8%; Orthodox 2.3%; other Christian 0.9%; Muslim 2.4%; unaffiliated 3.5%; other or unspecified 23%; none 10.1%

Currency   1 tolar (SIT) = 100 stotins

Gross domestic product   (2006) U.S. $43.08 billion

Gross domestic product per capita   (2006) U.S. $22,900

Life expectancy at birth   male 72.63 yr; female 80.29 yr

Major resources   lignite, lead, zinc, mercury, uranium, silver, hydropower, forests, apples, barley, bauxite, grapes/wine, hops, livestock, mercury, oats, pears, potatoes, rye, sugar beet, wheat

CROATIA

The mountainous Dalmatian coast runs the length of western Croatia. Inland, Croatia's landscape is characterised by further mountains, plateaus, rolling hills and fertile plains. The historic medieval city of Dubrovnik is separated from the rest of Croatia by a

The marina at Hvar, an island along the southern part of the rugged and beautiful Dalmatian coast, which is characterised by drowned alpine valleys creating steep islands and rocky peninsulas.

strip of land that gives Bosnia Herzegovina access to the sea. The coast has a Mediterranean climate, while inland the climate is more continental. Civil war virtually destroyed Croatia's tourist industry overnight, and only in the late 1990s did it show signs of recovery. The war caused considerable structural damage as well, and there were large-scale movements of refugees from Bosnia and within Croatia. International aid helped stabilise the economy, but the rebuilding process has been difficult and slow, although tourism is once again the chief foreign currency earner. Agricultural activity is mainly centred on the fertile Pannonian plain. Rich natural resources should help boost future prosperity, and the country is negotiating for EU membership.

NATIONAL DATA – CROATIA

Land area	56,414 sq km (21,782 sq mi)			
Climate		Temperatures		Annual precipitation
	Altitude m (ft)	January °C (°F)	July °C (°F)	mm (in)
Dubrovnik	49 (161)	9 (48)	25 (77)	1,037 (40.8)

Major physical features	highest point: Bobotov Kuk 2,522 m (8,274 ft); longest river: Sava (part) 940 km (584 mi)

Population	(2006 est.) 4,494,749

Form of government	multiparty republic with one legislative house

Armed forces	army 14,050; navy 2,500; air force 2,300

Capital city	Zagreb (691,724)

Official language	Croatian

Ethnic composition	Croat 89.6%; Serb 4.5%; other 5.9% (including Bosniak, Hungarian, Slovene, Czech and Roma)

Religious affiliations	Roman Catholic 87.8%; Orthodox 4.4%; other Christian 0.4%; Muslim 1.3%; other and unspecified 0.9%; none 5.2%

Currency	1 kuna (HRK) = 100 lipa

Gross domestic product	(2006) U.S. $59.41 billion

Gross domestic product per capita	(2006) U.S. $13,200

Life expectancy at birth	male 71.03 yr; female 78.53 yr

Major resources	oil, some coal, bauxite, low-grade iron ore, gypsum, natural asphalt, silica, mica, clays, salt, hydropower, corn, flax, fruits, grapes, oats, olives, potatoes, timber, wheat, tourism

BOSNIA AND HERZEGOVINA

Bosnia and Herzegovina declared independence from the former Yugoslavia in 1991, but were then devastated by the Serbian-dominated Federal Army in the civil war that followed. The country is rugged and

NATIONAL DATA – BOSNIA AND HERZEGOVINA

Land area 51,129 sq km (19,741 sq mi)

Climate	Altitude m (ft)	Temperatures		Annual precipitation mm (in)
		January °C (°F)	July °C (°F)	
Sarajevo	630 (2,067)	-1 (28)	19 (90)	931 (36.6)

Major physical features highest point: MaMaglic 2,386 m (7,828 ft); longest rivers: Sava (part) 940 km (584 mi), Bosna 241 km (150 mi)

Population (2006 est.) 4,498,976

Form of government multiparty republic with two legislative houses

Armed forces state army in transition 11,825

Largest cities Sarajevo (capital – 380,000); Banja Luka (165,100)

Official language Serbo-Croat

Ethnic composition Bosniak (Muslim) 48%; Serb 37.1%; Croat 14.3%; other 0.6%

Religious affiliations Muslim 40%; Orthodox 31%; Roman Catholic 15%; other 14%

Currency 1 marka (BAM or KM) = 100 fening

Gross domestic product (2006) U.S. $24.8 billion

Gross domestic product per capita (2006) U.S. $5,500

Life expectancy at birth male 74.39 yr; female 81.88 yr

Major resources coal, lignite, iron ore, bauxite, copper, lead, zinc, chromite, cobalt, manganese, nickel, clay, gypsum, salt, sand, forests, hydropower, apples, corn, grapes, livestock, mercury, olives, pears, plums, silver, sugar beet, tobacco, walnuts, wheat

The Turkish bridge at Mostar was built in 1566. It was destroyed in 1993–94 when the town was at the centre of fierce fighting between Bosnian Serbs and Croats.

mountainous, with only a 19-km (12-mi) strip of coastal access. In the north, near the border with Croatia, the Sava River forms a fertile plain. The southwest is dominated by a karst landscape of limestone plateaus. Alpine winds can make winters bitterly cold, although summers are generally mild. Agriculture is vital to the economy, with most of the fertile land in the north. Fruit, olives, rice, tobacco and grapes are grown, and vast timber reserves in the mountains form the basis of an important forestry industry. Sheep are also reared. The country has rich mineral resources, and coal, iron, copper, salt and zinc are mined extensively. The huge postwar problems of homelessness, refugees and mass unemployment have been slow to resolve, despite considerable financial aid. Industrial growth and modernisation have been slow, but reconstruction was helped by the introduction, in 1998, of a stable new Bosnian currency, the marka, now linked to the Euro.

SERBIA

Serbia is the largest of the former Yugoslav republics, formed after the breakup of Yugoslavia in 1991. It incorporates the previously independent regions of Vojvodina in the north and Kosovo in the south, and finally separated from Montenegro in 2006. Apart from the above two provinces, Serbia is almost entirely mountainous. The most fertile land is on the Pannonian plain, running from Hungary and Croatia into Vojvodina and northern Serbia. Several rivers, including the Sava, bisect this plain. Daravica, Serbia's highest peak, is in the mountains in the southwest. The climate is almost entirely continental. The rich Pannonian plain was once the breadbasket of Yugoslavia, and agriculture – especially cereal growing – remains important, employing about one-quarter of the population. In Kosovo farming is mostly subsistence orientated. Throughout the country vines are grown, and there is a significant forestry industry in the mountainous areas. Like other countries in the region, civil war and the international sanctions that followed damaged the economy. NATO airstrikes in 1999 destroyed much transportation infrastructure and industry, and an embargo on petroleum imports further hampered recovery. The issue regarding whether or not Kosovo becomes an independent state continues to be unresolved.

Belgrade, the capital of Serbia, viewed across the Danube River with the old Christian church in the foreground.

NATIONAL DATA – SERBIA

Land area 88,361 sq km (34,116 sq mi)

Climate	Altitude m (ft)	Temperatures January °C (°F)	July °C (°F)	Annual precipitation mm (in)
Belgrade	132 (433)	1 (45)	22 (63)	1,145 (45)

Major physical features highest point: Daravica 2,656 m (8,714 ft) in Prokletija Range on Albanian border

Population 9,396,411

Form of government republic

Armed forces no figures

Largest cities Belgrade (capital – 1,120,092); Novi Sad (191,405); Nis (173,724)

Official language Serbian

Ethnic composition Serb 66%; Albanian 17%; Hungarian 3.5%; other 13.5%

Religious affiliations Serbian Orthodox, Muslim, Roman Catholic, Protestant

Currency 1 new Yugoslav dinar (YUM) = 100 euro cents

Gross domestic product (2006) U.S. $44.83 billion

Gross domestic product per capita (2005) U.S. $4,400

Life expectancy at birth male 71 yr; female 76 yr

Major resources oil, gas, coal, iron ore, copper, lead, zinc, antimony, chromite, nickel, gold, silver, magnesium, pyrite, limestone, marble, salt, agricultural produce

MONTENEGRO

Part of the former Yugoslavia, Montenegro is a rugged, mountainous country with the Dinaric Alps running through it, and with several large rivers. Summers are hot and dry, while winters are mild and wet. Allied to Serbia for nearly 100 years, the country broke this link in 2006. The region had well-developed industrial and tourist bases, but was in ruins by 2000 following the civil war, with rising levels of organised crime. Montenegro remains largely agricultural, growing cereals and tobacco and rearing livestock such as pigs. Aluminium processing is the industrial mainstay.

NATIONAL DATA – MONTENEGRO

Land area 13,812 sq km (5,333 sq mi)

Climate	Altitude m (ft)	Temperatures January °C (°F)	July °C (°F)	Annual precipitation mm (in)
Podgorica	44 (144)	5 (41)	26 (79)	1,361 (53.5)

Major physical features highest point: Bobotov Peak 2,523 m (8,277 ft)

Population (2006 est.) 630,548

Form of government republic

Armed forces no figures

Capital city Podgorica (136,473)

Ethnic composition Montenegrin 43%; Serbian 32%; Bosniak (Muslim) 8%; Albanian 5%; other (Muslims, Croats, Roma) 12%

Religious affiliations Orthodox, Muslim, Roman Catholic

Currency 1 euro (EUR) = 100 euro cents

Gross domestic product (2006) U.S. $3.394 billion

Gross domestic product per capita (2005) U.S. $3,800

Life expectancy at birth no figures

Major resources bauxite, hydroelectricity

MACEDONIA

Macedonia came into being in 1991 following the breakup of Yugoslavia. A large part of the country is a high plateau 600 to 900 m (2,000–3,000 ft) above sea level, and the rest is mountainous. Civil war in the Balkans destabilised the country, and ethnic problems remain. International trade sanctions also damaged the economy. Many Macedonians find work abroad.

NATIONAL DATA – MACEDONIA

Land area 24,856 sq km (9,597 sq mi)

Climate	Altitude m (ft)	Temperatures January °C (°F)	July °C (°F)	Annual precipitation mm (in)
Skopje	673 (2,208)	2 (36)	23 (73)	508 (20)

Major physical features highest point: within Korab Mountains 4,634 m (15,203 ft); longest river: Po 620 km (380 mi); largest lake: Lake Garda 370 sq km (140 sq mi)

Population (2006 est.) 2,050,554

Form of government multiparty republic with one legislative house

Armed forces army 9,760; air force 1,130

Capital city Skopje (467,257)

Official language Macedonian

Ethnic composition Macedonian 64.2%; Albanian 25.2%; Turkish 3.9%; Roma 2.7%; Serb 1.8%; other 2.2%

Religious affiliations Macedonian Orthodox 64.7%; other Christian 0.37%; Muslim 33.3%; other and unspecified 1.63%

Currency 1 Macedonian denar (MKD) = 100 deni

Gross domestic product (2006) U.S. $16.91 billion

Gross domestic product per capita (2006) U.S. $8,200

Life expectancy at birth male 71.51 yr; female 76.62 yr

Major resources iron ore, copper, lead, zinc, chromite, manganese, nickel, tungsten, gold, silver, asbestos, gypsum, timber, antimony, arsenic, barley, maize (corn), cotton, livestock, potatoes, quartz, rice, rye, silicon, sunflowers, wheat

ALBANIA

Albania's mountainous geography and inaccessible coastal swamps have contributed to its isolation from Europe. The country's hardline government was the last communist regime in Europe to give way to popular pressure for reform, in the early 1990s. The collapse of the economy that followed was exacerbated by the later influx of Albanian Muslim and of Kosovan refugees. The country has struggled to modernise the economy and has experienced continuing emigration and a sharp decline in industrial output. The economy relies heavily on remittances from Albanians working abroad.

NATIONAL DATA – ALBANIA

Land area   27,398 sq km (10,578 sq mi)

Climate	Altitude m (ft)	Temperatures January °C (°F)	July °C (°F)	Annual precipitation mm (in)
Tirana	89 (292)	7 (45)	24 (75)	1,353 (53.2)

Major physical features   highest point: Mount Korabit 2,751 m (9,026 ft); longest river: Drin (part) 282 km (175 mi); largest lake: Lake Scutari 370 sq km (143 sq mi)

Population   (2006 est.) 3,581,655

Form of government   emergent democracy

Armed forces   army 16,000; navy 2,000; air force 3,500

Capital city   Tiranë (376,642); Elbasan (123,270); Durrës (116,275); Shkodër (109,604); Vlorë (104,118)

Official language   Albanian

Ethnic composition   Albanian 95%; Greek 3%; other 2% (Vlach, Roma, Serb, Macedonian, Bulgarian)

Religious affiliations   Muslim 70%; Albanian Orthodox 20%; Roman Catholic 10%

Currency   1 lek (ALL) = 100 qintars

Gross domestic product   (2006) U.S. $20.21 billion

Gross domestic product per capita   (2006) U.S. $5,600

Life expectancy at birth   male 74.78 yr; female 80.34 yr

Major resources   petroleum, natural gas, coal, bauxite, chromite, copper, iron ore, nickel, salt, timber, hydropower, asphalt, bitumen, cereals, cotton, grapes, olives, potatoes, tobacco

BULGARIA

Geographically, Bulgaria has a northern plateau and central lowlands separated by a mountain range, with another range to the southwest. Once one of the most acquiescent Soviet satellite states, since 1989 the country has abolished its centralised economy and has privatised land and industries. Farming, fishing, wine making and tourism are important, but petrochemicals and machinery earn most of Bulgaria's export revenue.

NATIONAL DATA – BULGARIA

Land area   110,550 sq km (42,684 sq mi)

Climate	Altitude m (ft)	Temperatures January °C (°F)	July °C (°F)	Annual precipitation mm (in)
Sofia	550 (1,804)	-1 (28)	20 (68)	571 (39)

Major physical features   highest point: Musala 2,925 m (9,596 ft); longest river: Danube (part) 2,850 km (1,771 mi)

Population   (2006 est.) 7,385,367

Form of government   multiparty republic with two legislative houses

Armed forces   army 25,000; navy 4,370; air force 13,100

Largest cities   Sofia (capital – 1,138,950); Plovdiv (341,464); Varna (312,026); Burgas (189,529)

Official language   Bulgarian

Ethnic composition   Bulgarian 83.9%; Turk 9.4%; Roma 4.7%; other 2% (including Macedonian, Armenian, Tatar, Circassian)

Religious affiliations   Bulgarian Orthodox 82.6%; Muslim 12.2%; other Christian 1.2%; other 4%

Currency   1 lev (BGL) = 100 stotinka

Gross domestic product   (2006) U.S. $77.13 billion

Gross domestic product per capita   (2006) U.S. $10,400

Life expectancy at birth   male 68.68 yr; female 76.13 yr

Major resources   bauxite, copper, lead, zinc, coal, timber, apples, barley, cattle, grapes, lignite, limestone, maize (corn), manganese, oil and natural gas, pigs, poultry, sheep, sunflowers, tobacco, uranium, wheat, tourism

ROMANIA

Romania is dominated by the Carpathian Mountains that run southeastwards before turning west towards Serbia; the highest peaks are in the southern Transylvanian Alps. Elsewhere, there are major rivers, plateaus and flat fertile plains. To the east a broad swampy delta leads to the Black Sea. The climate is mainly continental, with the mountains protecting western and southern areas from northeasterly winds.

NATIONAL DATA – ROMANIA

Land area	230,340 sq km (88,935 sq mi)			
Climate		Temperatures		Annual
	Altitude m (ft)	January °C (°F)	July °C (°F)	precipitation mm (in)
Bucharest	82 (269)	–2 (28)	22 (72)	595 (23.4)

Major physical features highest point: Mount Negoiu 2,535 m (8,317 ft); longest rivers: Danube (part) 2,850 km (1,771 mi) and Prut (part) 909 km (565 mi)
Population (2006 est.) 22,303,552
Form of government multiparty republic with two legislative houses
Armed forces army 66,000; navy 7,200; air force 14,000
Largest cities Bucharest (capital – 1,921,751); Iasi (321,580); Cluj-Napoca (318,027); Timisoara (317,651); Constanta (310,526); Craiova (302,622); Galati (298,584)
Official language Romanian
Ethnic composition Romanian 89.5%; Hungarian 6.6%; Roma 2.5%; Ukrainian 0.3%; German 0.3%; Russian 0.2%; Turkish 0.2%; other 0.4%
Religious affiliations Eastern Orthodox 86.8%; Protestant (denominations including Reformate and Pentecostal) 7.5%; Roman Catholic 4.7%; other (mainly Muslim) and unspecified 0.9%; none 0.1%
Currency 1 leu, plural lei (RON) = 100 bani
Gross domestic product (2006) U.S. $197.3 billion
Gross domestic product per capita (2006) U.S. $8,800
Life expectancy at birth male 68.14 yr; female 75.34 yr
Major resources petroleum, timber, natural gas, coal, lignite, iron ore, salt, hydropower, cereals, copper, fish, fruit, vegetables, grapes, gold, livestock, oil, potatoes, silver, sugar, uranium

From 1965 to 1989 Romania suffered under the repressive rule of Soviet-backed dictator Nicolae Ceausescu, who was eventually overthrown and executed following a popular revolt. Romania was saddled with a largely obsolete and polluting industrial base with which to begin the move from communism, resulting in political and economic troubles that further hampered development. Repeated attempts have been made to transform Romania into a free-market economy, but some of them have met with resistance – particularly where the closure of unprofitable industries might have an adverse effect on the local population. Some 45 percent of the population remains below the official poverty line, and many Romanians have emigrated to western Europe. Farming is still the cornerstone of the economy, although many rural communities were destroyed during the Ceausescu years. The main industries are machine building and metal processing.

Pine forests clad the limestone rocks of the Carpathian Mountains that sweep through Romania in a broad arc.

LATVIA

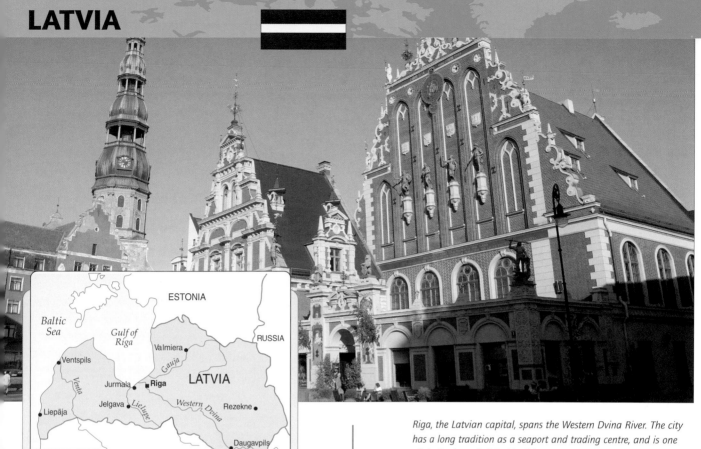

Riga, the Latvian capital, spans the Western Dvina River. The city has a long tradition as a seaport and trading centre, and is one of the busiest of all Baltic cities.

NATIONAL DATA - LATVIA

Land area 63,589 sq km (24,552 sq mi)

Climate	Altitude m (ft)	Temperatures January °C (°F)	July °C (°F)	Annual precipitation mm (in)
Riga	3 (10)	–5 (23)	17 (63)	633 (24.9)

Major physical features highest point: Vidzeme 311 m (1,020 ft); longest river: Western Dvina = Daugava (part) 1,060 km (635 mi)

Population (2006 est.) 2,274,735

Form of government multiparty republic with one legislative house

Armed forces army 1,817; navy 685; air force 255

Largest cities Riga (capital – 727,578); Daugavpils (109,482); Liepāja (85,915); Jelgava (66,087)

Official language Lettish

Ethnic composition Latvian 57.7%; Russian 29.6%; Belarusian 4.1%; Ukrainian 2.7%; Polish 2.5%; Lithuanian 1.4%; other 2%

Religious affiliations Lutheran, Roman Catholic, Russian Orthodox

Currency 1 Latvian lat (LVL) = 100 santims

Gross domestic product (2006) U.S. $35.08 billion

Gross domestic product per capita (2005) U.S. $15,400

Life expectancy at birth male 66.08 yr; female 76.85 yr

Major resources peat, limestone, dolomite, amber, hydropower, arable land, timber, paper-making industry, fish, flax, hydroelectric power, livestock, potatoes, rye, sugar beet, vegetables, wheat

The small, newly independent state of Latvia has much in common with the neighbouring republics of Estonia and Lithuania, although it is the poorest of the three. The country has a long sandy coastline, and inland the landscape consists of undulating plains rising in the east to a low plateau dotted with lakes and bogs. Forests and pastures cover much of the land, and there is abundant wildlife including lynx and European beavers. The climate is damp and cool.

The country gained independence from the former Soviet Union in 1991; because of massive immigration during the Soviet years, however, many Latvian citizens are of Russian descent. Heavily industrialised under the Soviets, Latvia produces pharmaceuticals, automobiles, machinery and other goods, but it relies on imported raw materials and fuel. Most trade is now with the EU, which Latvia joined in 2004. Agriculture has been redeveloped since independence, and products include grain, sugar beet and potatoes. Timber production and paper making are important industries, exploiting the country's forests. Cattle, pigs and poultry are the main farmed livestock. Latvia joined NATO in 2004.

LITHUANIA

Lithuania's terrain is low-lying, with sand dunes along the coast and lake-strewn hills in the southeast. The country became independent after the breakup of the Soviet Union in 1991. Lithuania maintained strong trading links with Russia after independence, which caused problems when the Russian economy went into recession in 1998. Foreign aid has been essential to allow Lithuania to rebuild its economy. Although 80 percent of businesses are now privatised, unemployment remains high. Lithuania joined the EU in 2004.

NATIONAL DATA – LITHUANIA

Land area 65,200 sq km (25,200 sq mi)

Climate	Altitude m (ft)	Temperatures January °C (°F)	July °C (°F)	Annual precipitation mm (in)
Rome	17 (56)	7 (45)	25 (77)	657 (25.9)

Major physical features highest point: Juozapine 292 m (958 ft); longest river: Neman (part) 963 km (582 mi)

Population (2006 est.) 3,585,906

Form of government multiparty republic with one legislative house

Armed forces army 10,100; navy 710; air force 1,200

Largest cities Vilnius (capital – 541,824); Kaunas (360,637); Klaipeda (187,316); Siauliai (129,037); Panevezys (115,315)

Official language Lithuanian

Ethnic composition Lithuanian 83.4%; Polish 6.7%; Russian 6.3%; other or unspecified 3.6%

Religious affiliations Roman Catholic 79%; Russian Orthodox 4.1%; Protestant (including Lutheran and Evangelical Christian Baptist) 1.9%; other or unspecified 5.5%; none 9.5%

Currency 1 litas (LTL) = 100 cents

Gross domestic product (2006) U.S. $54.03 billion

Gross domestic product per capita (2006) U.S. $15,100

Life expectancy at birth male 69.2 yr; female 79.49 yr

Major resources peat, amber, barley, fish, flax, legumes, livestock, potatoes, rye, sugar beet, timber, wheat

ESTONIA

Estonia is low-lying with pastureland, forests and marshes. It gained independence in 1991 following the breakup of the Soviet Union. The adoption of a new stable currency, wide-reaching privatisation and foreign investment have made Estonia the most successful of the Baltic states, with a fast-growing economy. The service sector employs two-thirds of the workforce, and industries include engineering and wood products.

NATIONAL DATA – ESTONIA

Land area 43,211 sq km (16,684 sq mi)

Climate	Altitude m (ft)	Temperatures January °C (°F)	July °C (°F)	Annual precipitation mm (in)
Tallinn	44 (144)	–5 (23)	17 (68)	676 (26.6)

Major physical features highest point: Munamägi 318 m (1,043 ft); largest lake: Lake Peipus (part) 3,548 sq km (1,370 sq mi)

Population (2006 est.) 1,324,333

Form of government multiparty republic with one legislative house

Armed forces army 3,429; navy 331; air force 193

Largest cities Tallinn (capital – 396,193); Tartu (101,740); Narva (66,936); Kohtla-Järve (45,740); Pärnu (44,198)

Official language Estonian

Ethnic composition Estonian 67.9%; Russian 25.6%; Ukrainian 2.1%; Belarusian 1.3%; Finn 0.9%; other 2.2%

Religious affiliations Evangelical Lutheran 13.6%; Orthodox 12.8%; other Christian (including Methodist, Seventh-Day Adventist, Roman Catholic, Pentecostal) 1.4%; unaffiliated 34.1%; other and unspecified 32%; none 6.1%

Currency 1 Estonian kroon (EEK) = 100 cents

Gross domestic product (2006) U.S. $26 billion

Gross domestic product per capita (2006) U.S. $19,600

Life expectancy at birth male 66.58 yr; female 77.83 yr

Major resources oil shale, peat, phosphorite, clay, limestone, sand, dolomite, sea mud, engineering, electronics, wood and wood products, textiles, tourism, cotton, fish, fruits, grains, livestock, potatoes, vegetables

BELARUS

This former Soviet republic consists largely of rolling plains, with one-third of the land covered by forests. Despite gaining independence in 1991 after the breakup of the Soviet Union, Belarus has maintained an unreconstructed Soviet system of politics and economics that has not encouraged foreign investment.

NATIONAL DATA – BELARUS

Land area	207,600 sq km (80,155 sq mi)			
Climate		Temperatures		Annual
	Altitude m (ft)	January °C (°F)	July °C (°F)	precipitation mm (in)
Minsk	234 (767)	-7 (19)	13 (55)	782 (30.7)

Major physical features highest point: Dzyarzhynsk Mountain 345 m (1,135 ft); longest river: Dnieper (part) 2,280 m (1,420 ft)

Population (2006 est.) 10,293,011

Form of government republic in name, although in fact a dictatorship

Armed forces army 29,600; navy 18,170; joint forces 25,170

Largest cities Minsk (capital – 1,765,800); Homyel (481,197); Mahilyow (366,900); Vitsyebsk (342,700); Hrodna (316,700); Brest (298,329)

Official language Belarusian, Russian

Ethnic composition Belarusian 81.2%; Russian 11.4%; Polish 3.9%; Ukrainian 2.4%; other 1.1%

Religious affiliations Eastern Orthodox 80%; other (including Roman Catholic, Protestant, Jewish and Muslim) 20%

Currency 1 Belarusian ruble (BYB/BYR) = 100 kopecks

Gross domestic product (2006) U.S. $80.74 billion

Gross domestic product per capita (2006) U.S. $7,800

Life expectancy at birth male 63.47yr; female 74.98 yr

Major resources timber/forests, peat deposits, oil, natural gas, granite, dolomitic limestone, marl, chalk, sand, gravel, clay, buckwheat, chloride, potassium, rye, sodium chloride, sugar beet, tobacco, wheat

MOLDOVA

Moldova is hilly, with rolling steppelands criss-crossed with deep ravines and forested slopes. This former Soviet republic gained independence in 1991 following the breakup of the Soviet Union. Moldova is the poorest country in Europe; by 2000 the economy had shrunk to only 40 percent of its size in the Soviet era. The country has almost no energy resources and relies upon Russia, to whom it has a large trading debt. The economy relies heavily on remittances from Moldovans working abroad.

NATIONAL DATA – MOLDOVA

Land area	33,371 sq km (12,885 sq mi)

Climate moderately continental

Major physical features highest point: Balaneshty 430 m (1,409 ft); longest river: Dneister (part) 1,420 km (880 mi)

Population (2006 est.) 4,466,706

Form of government multiparty parliamentary republic with one legislative house

Armed forces army 5,710; air force 1,040

Largest cities Chisinau (capital – 593,800); Tiraspol (157,000); Beltsy (122,700); Tighina (96,000); Ribnita (53,00)

Official language Moldovan

Ethnic composition Moldovan/Romanian 78.2%; Ukrainian 8.4%; Russian 5.8%; Gagauz 4.4%; Bulgarian 1.9%; other 1.3%

Religious affiliations Eastern Orthodox 98%; Jewish 1.5%; Baptist and other 0.5%

Currency 1 Moldovan leu (MDL) = 100 bani

Gross domestic product (2006) U.S. $8.971 billion

Gross domestic product per capita (2006) U.S. $2,000

Life expectancy at birth male 61.61 yr; female 69.88 yr

Major resources lignite, phosphorites, gypsum, limestone, barley, clay, corn, fruit, grapes, livestock, oil and natural gas, quartz sands, rye, soybeans, sugar beet, sunflowers, tobacco, vegetables, wheat

UKRAINE

The second most populous of the former Soviet republics after Russia, Ukraine also ranks second in terms of its economic resources. Ukraine achieved independence in 1991 after the breakup of the Soviet Union, but the path to democracy was hampered until the 'Orange Revolution' of 2004 brought reformism.

NATIONAL DATA – UKRAINE

Land area 603,700 sq km (233,100 sq mi)

Climate	Altitude m (ft)	Temperatures January °C (°F)	July °C (°F)	Annual precipitation mm (in)
Kiev	179 (587)	-5 (23)	20 (68)	643 (25.3)

Major physical features highest point: Hoverla 2,061 m (6,762 ft); longest river: Dnieper (part) 2,280 km (1,419 mi)

Population (2006 est.) 46,710,816

Form of government multiparty republic with one legislative house

Armed forces army 125,000; navy 13,500; air force 49,100

Largest cities Kiev (capital – 2,660,401); Kharkov (1,464,740); Dnepropetrovsk (1,056,497); ; Odessa (1,007,131); Donetsk (999,975); Zaporozhye (799,348)

Official language Ukrainian

Ethnic composition Ukrainian 77.8%; Russian 17.3%; Belarusian 0.6%; Moldovan 0.5%; Crimean Tatar 0.5%; Bulgarian 0.4%; Hungarian 0.3%; Romanian 0.3%; Polish 0.3%; Jewish 0.2%; other 1.8%

Religious affiliations Ukrainian Orthodox - Kiev Patriarchate 19%; Orthodox (no particular jurisdiction) 16%; Ukrainian Orthodox - Moscow Patriarchate 9%; Ukrainian Greek Catholic 6%; Ukrainian Autocephalous Orthodox 1.7%; Protestant, Jewish, none 38%

Currency 1 hryvnia (UAH) = 100 kopiykas

Gross domestic product (2006) U.S. $355.8 billion

Gross domestic product per capita (2006) U.S. $7,600

Life expectancy at birth male 64.71 yr; female 75.59 yr

Major resources iron ore, coal, manganese, natural gas, oil, salt, sulphur, graphite, titanium, magnesium, kaolin, nickel, mercury, timber, food processing, consumer goods, heavy engineering, chemicals and chemical equipment, asbestos, barley, corn, flax, gypsum, limestone, livestock, marble, ozocerite, peat, rye, sugar beet, tobacco, wheat

Geography

Ukraine's landscape features endless stretches of level steppe covering two-thirds of the country, broken by the Carpathian Mountains, which cross the southwest between the Slovak and Romanian borders. In the far south the Crimean Mountains overlook the south coast of the Crimean Peninsula, which divides the Black Sea from the Sea of Azov. Western Ukraine consists mainly of the Dnieper plateau, cut by deep valleys. East of the Dnieper, the land rises to low hills along the northeast border, and to the Azov Hills and the Donets Ridge in the southeast. The climate ranges from temperate continental in the northeast to Mediterranean on the south coast of the Crimea. Most forests are in the south and southwest mountains. Farther north, woodland alternates with bog and marsh, while a central band of woodland and steppe is largely given over to farmland. In the south, Askaniya Nova is one of the areas of virgin steppe designated as a nature reserve. Ukraine has a varied range of animal and plant life.

Society

Ukraine was at the heart of Kievan Rus, a powerful state in the 10th and 11th centuries, and the first Slav state. The cultural and religious legacies of Kievan Rus laid the foundations for later Ukrainian nationalism. In the 13th century Ukraine was overrun by Mongol and Tartar invaders. During the 14th century it came under the control of the Polish-Lithuanian crowns, aided by Cossacks recruited to defend the borders. The Cossacks declared a semi-independent state in 1648 and sought support from Russia, and during the 18th century much Ukrainian territory was absorbed into the Russian Empire. After the Russian Revolution of 1917, Ukraine enjoyed a period of independence, but in 1922 it was one of the four founder-republics of the Soviet Union. Ukraine endured huge hardship under the Stalinist regime in the 1930s in which more than 8 million died. A similar number were killed in World War II, and much of Ukraine's historic architecture and art was destroyed. Ukrainian nationalism, forced underground in the 1960s and 1970s, emerged again in the late 1980s.

The golden- domed Saint Mikhail's/Michael's Cathedral in Kiev, was demolished in 1937 and reconstructed between 1997-2000.

THE CHERNOBYL NUCLEAR DISASTER

In April 1986 a devastating accident – regarded as the worst in the history of nuclear power – occurred at the nuclear power plant at Chernobyl, 129 km (80 mi) north of Kiev. Caused, it is believed, by poor safety procedures, a chain reaction in the Number 4 reactor went out of control, creating explosions that blew off the reactor's heavy protective steel-and-concrete lid. Several workers in the immediate area were killed, and others died later after attempting to make the reactor safe again. More than 130,000 people had to be evacuated. A cloud of radioactive fallout drifted over large parts of the former Soviet Union, Europe and North America, causing more deaths and contaminating land and food produce.

Economy

A favourable climate and fertile soils meant that about one-half of all the agricultural output of the former Soviet Union came from Ukraine. Its huge mineral resources (coal, oil, iron ore and manganese) facilitated the production of a range of goods. After independence, however, the end of the Soviet trade system caused agricultural and industrial output to fall, and Ukraine faced a huge energy deficit, rampant inflation, and declining standards of living. Production fell by more than 50 percent in a decade, and by 2000 the only poorer European countries were Moldova and Albania.

Privatisation and other economic reforms have been slow and only partially successful, although initiatives such as selling off the state Kryvoryzhstal steelworks generated revenue to help overcome budget deficits. The lack of an efficient taxation system has resulted in poor levels of investment and unpaid wages in the public sector. There is a strong disparity in industrial growth: the east, which includes the ethnic Russian minority, is in recession, and growth is largely confined to the Ukrainian ethnic west and Kiev. Ferrous metals are Ukraine's main export. Other major industries include food processing, consumer goods, heavy engineering, chemicals and chemical equipment. Industry contributes 40 percent of GDP.

RUSSIA

Extending halfway around the northern hemisphere, Russia is the world's biggest country – almost twice the size of the United States. The country crosses 11 time zones and contains more than 20 autonomous republics and about 150 different ethnic groups. Much of this vast land is sparsely populated and thinly resourced.

NATIONAL DATA – RUSSIA

Land area   16,995,800 sq km (6,562,115 sq mi)

Climate	Altitude m (ft)	Temperatures January °C (°F)	July °C (°F)	Annual precipitation mm (in)
Moscow	156 (512)	-9 (45)	18 (63)	681 (26.8)
Sochi	31 (102)	7 (45)	23 (73)	1,351 (53.1)
Verkhoyansk	137 (449)	-51 (-60)	14 (57)	136 (5.3)

Major physical features   highest point: Elbrus 5,642 m (18,510 ft); longest river: Yenisei 4,129 km (2,566 mi)

Population   (2006 est.) 142,893,540

Form of government   federal multiparty republic with two legislative houses

Armed forces   army 395,000; navy 142,000; air force 160,000

Largest cities   Moscow (capital - 10,406,578); St. Petersburg (4,601,000); Novosibirsk (1,405,569); Yekaterinburg = Sverdlovsk (1,304,251); Nizhniy Novgorod = Gorky (1,297,550); Samara – Kuybyshev (1,151,681); Omsk (1,142,773); Kazan (1,110,022)

Official language   Russian

Ethnic composition   Russian 79.8%; Tatar 3.8%; Ukrainian 2%; Bashkir 1.2%; Chuvash 1.1%; other or unspecified 12.1%

Religious affiliations   Russian Orthodox 15–20%; Muslim 10–15%; other Christian 2%; non-affiliated 63%

Currency   1 Russian ruble (RUR) = 100 kopecks

Gross domestic product   (2006) U.S. $1.723 trillion

Gross domestic product per capita   (2006) U.S. $12,100

Life expectancy at birth   male 60.45 yr; female 74.1 yr

Major resources   oil, natural gas, coal, timber, antimony, asbestos, barley, basalt, bauxite, cobalt, copper, corn, diamonds, gas, gold, granite, iron ore, lead, livestock, marble, mercury, millet, molybdenum, nickel, oats, phlogopite, platinum, potassium salt, potatoes, rye, silver, sugar beet, sunflowers, tin, tobacco, tungsten, precious and semiprecious stones, vegetables, wheat, zinc

Geography

Russia can be divided into five main areas: the East European Plain, extending from the west to the Ural Mountains; the Urals; the West Siberian Plain between the Urals and the Yenisei River; the Central Siberian Plateau between the Yenisei and Lena Rivers; and the remote mountainous regions of Siberia. Within this huge land area are snow-capped mountains, volcanoes, thousands of miles of varied coastline, many islands, lakes and rivers, vast tracts of rolling grassland, frozen Arctic tundra, semideserts and forests of coniferous and broad-leaved trees. The climate is generally a cold continental type, although much warmer near the Black Sea and around Vladivostok. Winters are severe, falling as low as –70° C (–94° F) in northeast Siberia.

Animal life is varied, reflecting the many habitats and climatic zones, and ranges from Arctic species like walruses and seals to tigers, bears, cranes and eagles.

Society

For centuries Russia has influenced European and world history. The 1917 October Revolution ended the tsarist regime and heralded the formation of the communist Union of Soviet Socialist Republics (USSR) in 1922.

No longer the place where huge columns of Soviet military weaponry would be paraded each May Day, Red Square in Moscow still retains an air of history and grandeur. Seen here are part of the Kremlin (left) and St. Basil's Cathedral (right).

Following World War II the victorious Russians seized more territory in the east, and countries such as Poland, Czechoslovakia and Hungary became satellite states of the Soviet Empire. For the next 40 years or so, there followed the so-called Cold War – an ideological standoff between the West and the USSR, with the threat of nuclear war always present. In the late 1980s the USSR appeared to be relaxing its hardline stance, while countries in eastern Europe began to claim independence, and communist regimes toppled. By 1991, the great monolith of the USSR had dissolved, leaving 11 of the constituent republics, including Russia, to form the Commonwealth of Independent States (CIS).

Different types of federal subject (region) in the Russian Federation. Twenty-one republics (blue areas) enjoy autonomy on most issues. They correspond to some of Russia's many ethnic minorities. There are also 48 oblasts *(provinces), 7 krais (territories), 9 autonomous okrugs (districts) (green) and 1 autonomous* oblast *(pink).*

Economy

In the 1990s Russia struggled to establish a modern market economy, hampered by an entrenched bureaucracy and a dilapidated industrial base. Falling oil prices and a failing currency caused further setbacks, but a rise in oil prices has helped growth. Cereals form the major part of the agricultural sector, but only about one-tenth of the land is cultivated, most of it in the west, where the most suitable land for livestock rearing is found. Russia has the world's largest reserves of timber.

Heavy industry is the backbone of Russia's economy and draws on enormous resources of raw materials. The country also has vast energy reserves – of coal, oil and natural gas. Hydroelectric power is supplied by the Volga and Yenisei Rivers, but the nuclear power program was set back by the events of Chernobyl (see page 49). The economy remains overreliant on the export of commodities (accounting for 80 percent of exports), but these are vulnerable to swings in world prices. Goods and raw materials need to be carried over vast distances in Russia, and effective transportation links have been a major challenge since the abolition of central planning.

WHO ARE THE RUSSIANS?

More than 60 nationalities are contained within the Russian Federation, and they fall broadly into four main linguistic groups. The Indo-European group includes about 150 million Russian speakers and accounts for most of the population from the Baltic to the Pacific. The other three language groups are Finno-Ugric (mainly from the forest and tundra of the north and Balkans), the Turkic speakers of Asia and southeastern Europe, and the Caucasian group, encompassing languages spoken west of the Caucasus Mountains as well as some spoken east of the Caucasus, such as Chechen.

MALTA

Gozo, the second largest of the three islands that make up Malta. The commanding position they hold in the narrow straits between Sicily and Tunisia has long made them strategically important.

The islands of Malta are the peaks of a massive limestone outcrop stretching south from Sicily, dissected by bays and valleys. With little fresh water apart from rainfall, desalination plants are a necessity for a stable water supply. Natural vegetation is sparse because of centuries of overgrazing. Today only small mammals such as hedgehogs and bats are found, although bird species are more numerous. Malta has been occupied by Romans, Arabs, Christian feudal lords and the Knights of St. John. In 1814 it became a British colony. It gained independence in 1946, but in 1971 it swung towards the eastern bloc, ousted NATO forces and nationalised the dockyards. Efforts were made later to restore links with the West. Malta joined the EU in 2004.

Agriculture is restricted to terraced hillsides and lowlands. Vegetables, cereals and fruit are the main crops, and goats are the chief livestock. The economy depends largely on shipping and port facilities. The textile and garment industries, which generate the major exports, have suffered from EU import controls. Tourism is the main source of foreign exchange.

NATIONAL DATA – MALTA

Land area 316 sq km (122 sq mi)

Climate	Altitude m (ft)	Temperatures January °C (°F)	July °C (°F)	Annual precipitation mm (in)
Valleta	70 (230)	12 (54)	26 (79)	519 (20.4)

Major physical features largest island: Malta 246 sq km (95 sq mi); highest point: southwest cliffs 253 m (830 ft)

Population (2006 est.) 400,214

Form of government multiparty republic with one legislative house

Armed forces joint forces 2,237

Capital city Valletta (7,137)

Official language Maltese, English

Ethnic composition Maltese 95.7%; British 2.1%; others 2.2%

Religious affiliations Roman Catholic 98%; other 2%

Currency 1 euro (EUR) = 100 euro cents

Gross domestic product (2006) U.S. $8.122 billion

Gross domestic product per capita (2006) U.S. $20,300

Life expectancy at birth male 76.83 yr; female 81.31 yr

Major resources limestone, salt, tourism, port facilities, fruit, goats, pigs, poultry, tobacco, vegetables, wheat

VATICAN CITY

The last remnant of the former Papal States, the Vatican City, on the west bank of the Tiber River, is enclosed by the city of Rome. The world's smallest state, it is the headquarters of the Roman Catholic church, which refused to be incorporated into the Italian nation in 1860. Vatican City consists solely of the buildings housing the church's administration and other functions. Other buildings under Vatican control include the summer palace at Castel Gandolfo outside Rome. Vatican City has no independent economy, although it has its own radio station, banking, postal and telephone systems, and strong tourist and publishing industries. The church's assets – priceless art, real estate and gold reserves – make it extremely wealthy.

NATIONAL DATA – VATICAN CITY

Land area	0.44 sq km (0.17 sq mi)		
Climate	Temperatures January °C (°F)	July °C (°F)	Annual precipitation mm (in)
	8 (46)	23 (73)	724 (28.5)

Major physical features	none
Population	(2004 est.) 780
Form of government	city-state with one appointed absolute ruler – the pope
Armed forces	Swiss Guard 100
Official language	Italian
Official religion	Roman Catholicism
Religious affiliations	Roman Catholic 100%
Currency	1 Vatican lira (VL) = 1 euro (EUR) = 100 euro cents
Major resources	tourism

SAN MARINO

San Marino, in central Italy, is the second smallest republic in the world, and has been independent since it was founded in the 4th century. An enclave of the Apennine Mountains, San Marino declined to become part of Italy in 1861, although the economic and cultural links between the two countries have remained strong. Cattle are reared on mountain pastures, and the lower slopes are cultivated with vines. The majority of San Marino's raw materials for light industries – such as clothing, electronics and ceramics – come from Italy, as does its power supply. Many of San Marino's students attend Italian universities. Although many of its people have emigrated, chiefly to Italy and the United States, a large number of Italians have settled in San Marino. Tourism is the main source of revenue, enabling the republic to remain an independent state.

NATIONAL DATA – SAN MARINO

Land area	61 sq km (24 sq mi)
Climate	mediterranean
Major physical features	highest point: Monte Titano (capital on its slopes) 739 m (2,424 ft)
Population	(2006 est.) 29,251
Form of government	multiparty republic with one legislative house
Capital city	San Marino (2,294)
Official language	Italian
Ethnic composition	Sammarinesi 84.9%; Italian 14.6%; others 0.5%
Religious affiliations	Roman Catholic 95.2%; nonreligious 3%; others 1.8%
Currency	1 euro (EUR) = 100 euro cents
Gross domestic product	(2001) U.S. $940 million
Gross domestic product per capita	(2001) U.S. $34,600
Life expectancy at birth	male 78.23 yr; female 85.5 yr
Major resources	building stone, cattle, dairy products, olives, vines, wheat, tourism

ITALY

Italy has one of the oldest histories in Europe, second only to Greece. It is also one of Europe's youngest unified states. The rural landscape is spectacular, and the country's long cultural history has left a legacy of ruined temples and classical sculptures, medieval castles and fine Renaissance churches and paintings.

NATIONAL DATA – ITALY

Land area 294,020 sq km (181,252 sq mi)

Climate		Temperatures		Annual
	Altitude m (ft)	January °C (°F)	July °C (°F)	precipitation mm (in)
Rome	17 (56)	8 (46)	23 (73)	724 (28.5)

Major physical features highest point: Monte Rosa 3,505 m (11,500 ft); longest river: Po 652 km (405 mi); largest lake: Lake Garda 370 sq km (143 sq mi)

Population (2006 est.) 58,133,509

Form of government multiparty republic with two legislative houses

Armed forces army 112,000; navy 34,000; air force 45,152

Largest cities Rome (capital – 2,547,677); Milan (1,308,735); Naples (984,242); Turin (900,608); Palermo (670,820); Genoa (620,316); Bologna (373,473); Florence (366,901)

Official language Italian

Ethnic composition Italian 94.1%; Sardinian 2.7%; Rhaetian 1.3%; others 1.9%

Religious affiliations Roman Catholic 90%; Protestant and Jewish communities and growing Muslim immigrant community

Currency 1 euro (EUR) = 100 euro cents

Gross domestic product (2006) U.S. $1.727 trillion

Gross domestic product per capita (2006) U.S. $29,700

Life expectancy at birth male 76.88 yr; female 82.94 yr

Major resources coal, hydroelectric power, mercury, zinc, potash, marble, barite, asbestos, pumice, fluorspar, feldspar, pyrite (sulphur), natural gas and crude oil reserves, fish, cereals, citrus fruits, grapes/wine, iron ore, livestock, olives, potatoes, sugar, vegetables, tourism

Geography

Italy is shaped like a boot, with the island of Sicily near the toe. To the west is Sardinia, the largest island in the Mediterranean. In the north Italy is separated from the rest of Europe by the Alps. Southwards, beyond the fertile expanse of the great northern plain, are the Apennines, which form a rocky backbone from the Alps in the northwest to Calabria in the toe of the peninsula. Spectacular lakes such as Maggiore and Como in the north are water-filled valleys scooped out by glacial action. The coastline is extremely varied and is perhaps at its most spectacular along the steep cliffs of the Amalfi coast near Ravello. Earth tremors and volcanic activity are common in Italy.

The climate in the north is cool in summer and cold in winter. Farther south it is typically Mediterranean, with sunny summers and mild winters. Vegetation in the south is typically shrub-supporting scrubland; crops dominate the northern plain, while oak, chestnut and

beech forests grow in the Apennines. Bears, chamois, wolves, alpine rabbits and other mountain-dwelling species can still be found.

Society

Italy was once the power base of the mighty Roman Empire, the birthplace of the Catholic church, and the cradle of the Renaissance. Its literary tradition goes back almost unbroken to Roman times. Among its great artists are Leonardo da Vinci (1452–1519) and Raphael (1483–1520).

Economy

Italy's dependence on imports of food and energy has created a large balance-of-trade deficit. Although 65 percent of available land is farmed, much of it is in

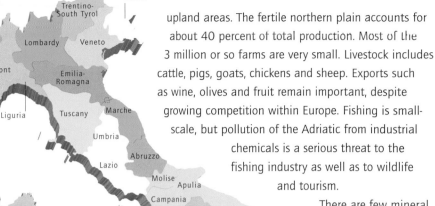

upland areas. The fertile northern plain accounts for about 40 percent of total production. Most of the 3 million or so farms are very small. Livestock includes cattle, pigs, goats, chickens and sheep. Exports such as wine, olives and fruit remain important, despite growing competition within Europe. Fishing is small-scale, but pollution of the Adriatic from industrial chemicals is a serious threat to the fishing industry as well as to wildlife and tourism.

There are few mineral resources in Italy, although oil deposits in Sicily provide about 6 percent of the country's energy needs; however, up to 80 percent of Italy's energy is imported. The national Energy Plan, whereby energy would be both conserved and generated by nuclear power and coal, has yet to be properly implemented. Hydroelectricity provides half of the power requirements in northern Italy. Manufacturing employs over one-fifth of the workforce, largely in the north. Automobiles, fashion items (especially clothes and shoes) and chemicals are important export commodities. Italy's climate, landscape, food and culture attract more than 20 million tourists each year, providing employment to many and a valuable influx of foreign currency. Italy is a member of the EU.

The city of Florence in northern Italy is renowned for its superb Renaissance architecture, museums and churches. The duomo, *or* cathedral, *dominates the city.*

THE RESTLESS EARTH BENEATH ITALY

Italy lies on the boundary between the Eurasian and the African tectonic plates, where earth tremors are common. In Sicily, Etna is Europe's highest active volcano at 3,323 m (10,902 ft); at night the glow of molten lava from its crater is visible for miles. Other volcanoes include Stromboli in the Lipari islands, and Vesuvius near Naples, which famously erupted in 79 A.D. The uplands near Rome are also volcanic, and there are mud springs at Viterbo. Thermal springs rise as far north as the Phlegraean Fields near Padua. The whole region is subject to occasional severe earthquakes.

GREECE

The flowering of art, literature and thought that took place in the city-states of Greece between the 8th and 5th centuries B.C. has been a major influence on the development of European culture and civilisation. Today the country is world-famous for its rich cultural heritage – particularly its architecture and sculpture – as well as for its great natural beauty.

Geography

Greece is a land of peninsulas and island chains formed by parallel mountain ranges that were flooded by the rising levels of the Mediterranean Sea. Its coastline is deeply indented with bays and inlets. The whole region is geologically unstable and experiences frequent tremors. Mainland Greece forms the southern end of the Balkan Peninsula. The steep Rhodope Mountains form a barrier in the north, and the Pindus Mountains in the northwest form a

NATIONAL DATA - GREECE

Land area	130,800 sq km (50,502 sq mi)			

Climate	Altitude m (ft)	Temperatures January °C (°F)	July °C (°F)	Annual precipitation mm (in)
Athens	107 (351)	9 (48)	28 (82)	424 (16.6)

Major physical features highest point: Olympus 2,917 m (9,570 ft); longest rivers: Vardar (part) 388 km (241 mi) and Aliàkmon 314 km (195 mi)

Population (2006 est.) 10,688,058

Form of government multiparty republic with one legislative house

Armed forces army 110,000; navy 19,250; air force 23,000

Largest cities Athens (capital – 745,514); Salonika (363,987); Piraeus (175,697); Pátrai (161,114)

Official language Greek

Ethnic composition Greek 98%; other 2%

Religious affiliations Greek Orthodox 98%; Muslim 1.3%; other 0.7%

Currency 1 euro (EUR) = 100 euro cents

Gross domestic product (2005) U.S. $236.8 billion

Gross domestic product per capita (2005) U.S. $22,200

Life expectancy at birth male 76.72 yr; female 81.91 yr

Major resources lignite, petroleum, iron ore, bauxite, lead, zinc, nickel, magnesite, marble, salt, hydropower potential, barytes, chrome, cotton, fruit, vegetables, grapes/wine, livestock, olives, sugar beet, tobacco, wheat, tourism

central ridge running down to the Aegean Sea –
producing an archipelago of more than 2,000 islands,
of which Crete is the largest. Only 10 percent of these
islands are inhabited but they make up one-fifth of
Greece's total land area. In the south is the
mountainous plateau of the Peloponnese. Separated
from the northern mainland by the Corinth Canal that
links the Aegean and Ionian Seas, the Peloponnese
extends into four rocky peninsulas. The Mediterranean
climate varies according to region: the northeast gets
snow on the mountains in winter, while in the south
warm winds make winters mild. Summers are hot and
dry, and hot, arid winds intensify the heat in Crete and
the southern islands.

Clearing and grazing have reduced the original
forest cover to one-fifth of the land area, mainly in the
north. Scrubland predominates in cleared lowland areas
in the Peloponnese. Corfu and Levkas have lush
vegetation. The northern forests shelter some large
mammals that are scarce elsewhere in Europe, such as
bears, wolves and lynx. There are also many reptile
species in the south, including chameleons.

Society

Between 2000 and 1500 B.C. Crete was the centre of
the Minoan civilisation, usually considered Europe's
earliest. It is thought that the Greek city-states, such as
Athens, may have originated in about 1200 B.C.
Literature, art, architecture, philosophy and politics
flourished. This rich civilisation reached its peak around
the 5th century B.C, but rivalries between the city-states
weakened them, and they were taken over by Philip II of
Macedonia (382–336 B.C.). His son, Alexander the Great
(356–323 B.C.), spread Greek culture across Asia to
India. But by the end of the 3rd century B.C. Greece had
succumbed to the rising power of Rome. After the 4th
century A.D. Greece had become part of the Byzantine
Empire ruled from Constantinople, and in 1460, after
the fall of Constantinople, most of Greece came under
the control of the Ottoman Empire. In 1830, after a
fierce struggle, an independent Greek state was
established in the Peloponnese, central Greece and the

*A characteristic whitewashed church bell-tower and windmill on the
Greek island of Thira (formerly Santorini) in the Aegean Sea.*

Aegean, with other islands added later. Occupation by
the Nazis in World War II was followed by civil war and
a military coup, but under a constitution of 1975,
democratic elections were restored.

Economy

Greece is one of the poorer countries in the EU. Greek
trade has increased within the EU, and Greece has
benefited from agricultural subsidies, but low-value
exports and high-value imports have created a growing
trade deficit. Services, especially tourism, banking and
shipping, are the most profitable sector. Agriculture
employs 18 percent of the workforce, but productivity is
low. Only one-quarter of the land is cultivated, and
many farmers still rely on draft animals. Crops include
cotton, tobacco, olives and citrus fruits. Sheep and goats
are raised throughout the country. Fishing is a small-
scale industry.

Greece has some mineral resources, but most raw
materials are imported, including about 75 percent of
fuel needs. There are plans to produce energy from
hydroelectricity and by converting power stations fired
by oil to locally available lignite and peat. Most
industry is centred on Athens. Manufactured goods
include cigarettes, textiles, clothing, cement and
fertiliser. The shipping industry is one of the world's
largest and accounts for more than 30 percent of the
income from services. Tourism provides foreign exchange
as well as jobs in service and construction industries.

GOVERNMENT IN GREECE

Greece is governed by a single-chamber parliament of
300 members. The leader of the majority party becomes
prime minister and head of government. The president
is elected by parliament for a five-year term and is
supreme commander of the armed forces. Governments
in Greece are elected for a four-year term, and all Greek
citizens who are over the age of 18 are required to vote.
Greece's administrative regions are divided into 51
departments. Mayors and councils are elected locally
but are funded by the national government. Greece is a
member of NATO and of the EU.

CYPRUS

The third largest island in the Mediterranean, Cyprus is a former British colony that gained independence in 1960. It is divided by a long-running conflict between the majority Greek population in the south and the minority Turkish population in the north, separated by a UN-operated buffer zone. On the north coast are the Kyrenia Mountains, and in the south, the Troodos. The fertile Mesaoria plain in the centre is the site of Nicosia. Summers are hot and dry, while winter is the rainy season. Scrubland predominates; the former extensive woodlands are now found only in the mountains. Much of the wildlife has been overhunted, and fishing is poor. Crops include wheat, barley, citrus fruits, potatoes, tobacco, grapes, olives, almonds and vegetables.

Cyprus's economic expansion, funded by foreign aid, was severely hampered by the Turkish invasion of 1974. Most factories came under Turkish control, but the Turkish sector still relies on agriculture and support from Turkey. The Greek sector has enjoyed impressive growth in industry and tourism. The Turkish Republic of Northern Cyprus, proclaimed in 1983, is only recognised by Turkey. Negotiations for Cyprus to be reunified ended without settlement in 2004. Cyprus joined the EU in 2004, although EU laws do not apply to areas of the island under the control of Turkish Cypriots.

A Cypriot church. Four-fifths of Cypriots are of Greek descent, and almost all Greek Cypriots belong to the Greek Orthodox church.

NATIONAL DATA – CYPRUS

Land area	9,240 sq km (3,568 sq mi)			

Climate	Altitude m (ft)	Temperatures January °C (°F)	July °C (°F)	Annual precipitation mm (in)
Nicosia	175 (574)	10 (50)	29 (84)	355 (13.9)

Major physical features	highest point: Mount Olympus 1,951 m (6,403 ft)

Population	(2006 est.) 784,301

Form of government multiparty republic with one legislative house (Turkish republic not recognised internationally)

Armed forces national guard 10,000

Largest cities Nicosia (capital – 202,488); Limassol (156,286); Larnaka (70,000); Famagusta (43,975)

Official language Greek, Turkish

Ethnic composition Greek 77%; Turkish 18%; other 5%

Religious affiliations Greek Orthodox 78%; Muslim 18%; Maronite, Armenian Apostolic and other 4%

Currency 1 euro (EUR) = 100 euro cents; 1 Turkish New lira (YTL) = 100 kurus

Gross domestic product (2006) Republic of Cyprus: U.S. $17.79 billion; north Cyprus: U.S. $4.54 billion

Gross domestic product per capita (2005) Republic of Cyprus: U.S. $22,700; (2004) north Cyprus: U.S. $7,135

Life expectancy at birth male 75.44 yr; female 80.31 yr

Major resources copper, pyrites, asbestos, gypsum, timber, salt, marble, tourism, almonds, beans, carob, citrus fruits, chromium, clay, grapes/wine, iron ore, olives, potatoes, vegetables, barley, wheat

Gibraltar is a huge ridge of limestone rock 6.5 sq km (2.5 sq mi) in extent, seen here from La Linea in Spain on the Costa del Sol.

FAROE ISLANDS

The Faroes are a group of 22 islands in the Atlantic between Scotland and Iceland, 18 of which are inhabited. The landscape is harsh and rugged, with high coastal cliffs and treacherous straits between islands. The North Atlantic Drift brings mild winters and cool summers. Trees survive only where sheltered from the strong winds. Wildlife consists of seals and seabirds including puffins and eider, valued for their feathers. There are no native mammals apart from the seals, but rats and mice were introduced by early settlers, and Vikings brought sheep in the 9th century.

The islands came under Norwegian rule in 1035 and passed to Denmark in 1380. In 1948 a growing nationalist movement led to the Faroes becoming a self-governing dependency of Denmark, although they are pressing for independence. One-third of the population lives around the main harbour and capital, Thorshavn. Woollen yarns and knitted garments are produced by the islanders, but fishing and associated industries are more important, providing 95 percent of exports. Whaling is carried out, despite international concern. Agriculture is mainly grass for fodder and vegetables. Hydroelectricity provides all energy needs.

GIBRALTAR

Gibraltar is a small, self-governing British colony that occupies the southern tip of Spain, to which it is joined by a low sandy isthmus. Gibraltar rises steeply to 425 m (1,394 ft) and has many fortifications from all periods of its history. There are no rivers or springs, so rainwater catchment reservoirs occupy a large area of the summit. There is almost no rain in the hot summer.

The word Gibraltar derives from the Arabic *Jabr al-Tariq*, named for a Moorish emir, Tariq ibn Ziyad, who captured it in 711. It remained under Muslim rule until 1462. Captured by the British in 1704, it became a strategic base and remains so today. Spain lays claim to Gibraltar, but Gibraltarians – who are a mixture of Moorish, Maltese, Spanish, Genoese, British and Jewish descent – have always voted overwhelmingly to remain British. One-third of the population is made up of resident foreigners, and Spaniards cross daily to work on 'the rock'. The colony's economy depends largely on the extensive port facilities and on light manufacturing, banking and finance. Tourism is increasingly important and is served by the airport close to the Spanish border.

DEPENDENCIES IN EUROPE

CHANNEL ISLANDS

The Channel Islands are a group of small islands in the English Channel off the northwest coast of France. They have been British crown dependencies since the Norman Conquest of 1066. The Channel Islands divide into two self-governing Bailiwicks: Jersey (the island of Jersey) and Guernsey (all other islands including Guernsey, Alderney, Herm and Sark). They were the only British soil occupied by German troops in World War II.

The climate is temperate, with cool summers and mild winters. The resident population is a mix of people of British and French descent. English is the dominant language, although many people speak French.

Jersey is the southernmost and largest of the Channel Islands, with a land area of 117 sq km (45 sq mi). The coastline combines sandy beaches and low rugged hills. Inland there are rolling plains. St. Helier, the capital, has a harbour, shops, restaurants and hotels. About 30 percent of the population is concentrated in St. Helier. Evidence remains of the German occupation, including fortifications and an underground hospital intended to treat wounded German soldiers.

Jersey's main income is derived from financial services such as banking and insurance, but agricultural exports (chiefly milk, potatoes, tomatoes and flowers) are also important, as is light industry such as textiles and electronics. Tourism accounts for about 25 percent of GDP.

Guernsey, the second largest island after Jersey, is about 65 sq km (25 sq mi) in area. The principal town is St. Peter Port, a deepwater harbour popular with visiting yachts, and an important sea ferry port. Guernsey also has an airport. The island's main income is from financial services such as banking, insurance and fund management; these represent 55 percent of income. The region in general is also a tax haven thanks to its light tax and death duties. Tourism is important but is declining, as are the traditional horticultural activities such as flower and vegetable growing. Alderney is about 7.7 sq km

The Laxey Wheel on the Isle of Man, built in 1854, pumped water from the Laxey iron ore mines in the Agneash Valley. It is the largest of its kind in the world.

(3 sq mi) in area. The fertile soil supports an agricultural industry based on potato and cereal growing. Dairy farming is also important. Alderney's principal town is St. Anne.

ISLE OF MAN

Lying in the Irish Sea between the northwest coast of England, the south coast of Scotland and the east coast of Northern Ireland, the Isle of Man is not part of the United Kingdom but a virtually self-governing crown possession. It is about 48 km (30 mi) long with a rocky coastline enclosing a central highland area. Low-lying land on either side is used to cultivate potatoes and cereals. There are signs of Neolithic settlements as early as 2000 B.C., and Celts and Vikings are among other settlers. It came under English control in the 15th century, and since 1828 the island has been administered by a governor appointed by the monarch. The island's chief industry is tourism, and its Tourist Trophy (TT) motorcycle races attract many visitors. It is also known for its tailless Manx cats.

The Spitsbergen island group lies in the Arctic Ocean about 580 km (360 mi) north of Norway. The largest island, Spitsbergen, covers an area of 39,000 sq km (15,060 sq mi).

SVALBARD AND JAN MAYEN ISLANDS

Svalbard, a bleak Arctic archipelago north of Norway, was recognised as a Norwegian possession in 1920. It contains the Spitsbergen group, as well as White Island, King Charles Land and Bear Island. Well known to the Vikings, the islands were at first a centre for whaling and later hunting. Since 1773 they have been used as a base for explorations to the North Pole. The discovery of coal in the early 20th century brought the islands to prominence. The 1920 treaty that recognised Norwegian sovereignty over the islands shared mineral rights with several other nations, but by the 1990s only Norway and Russia continued to mine coal there.

Jan Mayen island off the northeast coast of Greenland was annexed by Norway in 1929. Named for a 17th-century seafarer, it is a bleak volcanic island, dominated by the extinct volcano Beerenberg. It supports only scant wildlife and is used as a radio and navigational station.

GLOSSARY

Words in SMALL CAPITALS refer to other entries in the Glossary.

Amerindian A member of one of the many INDIGENOUS PEOPLES of Central and South America.

Anglican A member of the PROTESTANT church—founded in England in the 16th century—including the Church of England and other churches throughout the world.

apartheid A way of organising society to keep racial groups apart. Introduced after 1948 in South Africa by the National Party to ensure continued white political dominance, it has now been dismantled.

Buddhism A religion founded in India in the 6th and 5th centuries B.C. and based on the teachings of Gautama Siddhartha (c. 563–483 B.C.), the Buddha, or 'Awakened One'.

cereal A cultivated grass selectively bred to produce high yields of edible grain for consumption by humans and livestock. The most important are wheat (*Triticum*), rice (*Oryza sativa*) and maize/corn (*Zea mays*).

Christianity A religion based on the teachings of Jesus Christ and originating from JUDAISM in the 1st century A.D. Its main beliefs are found in the Bible, and it is now the world's most widespread religion, divided into a number of churches and sects, including ROMAN CATHOLICISM, PROTESTANTISM and ORTHODOX CHURCHES.

Communism A social and economic system based on the communal ownership of property. It usually refers to the STATE-controlled social and economic systems in the former Soviet Union and Soviet bloc countries and in the People's Republic of China.

Confucianism A religion or moral code based on the teachings of the Chinese philosopher Confucius (c. 551–479 B.C.) that formed the foundations of Chinese imperial administration and ethical behavior; also followed in Korea and other east Asian countries.

constitution The fundamental statement of laws that defines the way a country is governed.

constitutional monarchy A form of government with a hereditary head of STATE or monarch and a CONSTITUTION.

democracy A form of government in which policy is made by the people (direct democracy) or on their behalf (indirect democracy). Indirect democracy usually takes the form of competition among political parties at elections.

Dependency (1) A territorial unit under the jurisdiction of another STATE but not formally annexed to it. **(2)** An unequal economic or political relationship between two states or groups of states, in which one side is dependent on and supports the other.

ethnic group A group of people sharing a social or cultural identity based on language, religion, customs and/or common descent or kinship.

EU (European Union) An alliance of European NATIONS formed to agree common policies in the areas of trade, aid, agriculture and economics.

exports Goods or services sold to other countries.

federalism A form of CONSTITUTIONAL government in which power is shared between two levels – a central, or federal, government and a tier of provincial or STATE governments.

GDP (Gross Domestic Product) The total value of a country's annual output of goods and services with allowances made for depreciation.

Hinduism A religion originating in India in the 2nd millennium B.C. It emphasises mystical contemplation and ascetic practices that are closely interwoven with much of Indian culture.

indigenous peoples The original inhabitants of a region.

Islam A religion based on the revelations of God to the prophet Muhammad in the 7th century A.D., as recorded in the Qu'ran. It teaches submission to the will of God and is practiced throughout the Middle East, North Africa and parts of Southeast Asia.

Judaism A religion that developed in ancient Israel based on God's law and revelations declared to Moses on Mount Sinai.

Methodism A PROTESTANT denomination of the CHRISTIAN church based on the teachings of the English theologian John Wesley (1703–91).

monarch A form of rule where there is a hereditary head of STATE.

Muslim An adherent of ISLAM.

nation A community that believes it consists of a single people, based on historical and cultural criteria.

nation-state A STATE in which the inhabitants all belong to one NATION. Most states claim to be nation-states; in practice almost all of them include minority groups.

Native American The INDIGENOUS PEOPLES of North America.

official language The language used by governments, schools, courts and other official institutions in countries where the population has no single common mother tongue.

one-party state A political system in which there is no competition to the government party at elections, as in COMMUNIST and military regimes.

parliamentary democracy A political system in which the legislature (Parliament) is elected by all the adult members of the population and the government is formed by the party that commands a majority in the Parliament.

Protestant Term describing CHRISTIAN denominations that share a common rejection of the authority of the pope as head of the church, and of many ROMAN CATHOLIC practices.

Roman Catholic The largest of the CHRISTIAN churches, headed by the pope in Rome. It traces its origin and authority to St. Peter, one of the disciples of Jesus Christ and the first bishop of Rome. There are believers on all continents.

Shi'ite Muslim A member of the smaller of the two main divisions of ISLAM. Followers recognise Muhammad's son-in-law, Ali, and his descendants, the imams (prayer leaders), as his true successors and legitimate leaders of Islam.

state The primary political unit of the modern world, usually defined by its possession of sovereignty over a territory and its people.

subtropical The climatic zone between the TROPICS and TEMPERATE zones. There are marked seasonal changes of temperature but it is never very cold.

Sunni Muslim A member of the larger of the two main divisions of ISLAM. Its members recognise the Caliphs as the successors to Muhammad and follow the *sunna*, or way of the prophet, as recorded in the *hadithw*, the teachings of Muhammad.

temperate climate Any one of the climatic zones in mid-latitudes, with a mild climate. They cover areas between the warm TROPICS and cold polar regions.

tropics (tropical) The area between the Tropic of Cancer (23°30'N) and the Tropic of Capricorn (23°30'S), marking the lines of latitude farthest from the equator where the Sun is still found directly overhead at midday in midsummer.

FURTHER REFERENCES

General Reference Books

Allen, J. L., *Student Atlas of World Geography*, McGraw-Hill, Maidenhead, 2007.

Atlas of the World, Philip's, London, 2007.

Brazier, C. and Hamed, A., *The World Guide: Global Reference Country by Country*, New Internationalist Publications Ltd, Market Harborough, 2007.

Clawson, D. L., et al, *World Regional Geography*, Prentice Hall, Harlow, 2006.

de Blij, H. J. and P. O. Muller, *Concepts and Regions in Geography*, John Wiley & Sons, Chichester, 2004.

Johnston, R. J., Taylor, P. J. and Watts, M. J., *Geographies of Global Change: Remapping the World*, Blackwell, Oxford, 2002.

Muller, P. O. and E. Muller-Hames, *Geography, Study Guide: Realms, Regions, and Concepts*, John Wiley & Sons, Chichester, 2005.

Oxford Atlas of the World, Oxford University Press, Oxford, 2007.

Parsons, J. (ed.), *Geography of the World*, DK Children, London and New York, 2006.

Warf, B. (ed.), *Encyclopedia of Human Geography*, Sage Publications, London and New York, 2006.

Specific to this volume

Bideleux, R. and Jeffries, I., *A History of Eastern Europe: Crisis and Change*, Routledge, Oxford, 2007.

Davies, N., *Europe: A History*, Pimlico, 1997.

Forsyth, J., *A History of the Peoples of Siberia*, Cambridge University Press, Cambridge, 2006.

Glenny, M., *The Balkans, 1804-1999: Nationalism, War and the Great Powers*, Granta Books, London, 2000.

Graham, B., *In Search of Ireland: A Cultural Geography*, Routledge, London, 1997.

Hancock, M. D. et al, *Politics in Europe: An Introduction to the Politics of the United Kingdom, France, Germany, Russia, Italy, Sweden and the European Union*, Palgrave Macmillan, Basingstoke, 2002.

Helle, K. (ed.), *The Cambridge History of Scandinavia*, Cambridge University Press, Cambridge, 2003.

Jude, T., *The Serbs: History, Myth and the Destruction of Yugoslavia*, Yale University Press, New Haven, CT, 2000.

Kaplan, M., *The Portuguese: The Land and Its People*, Carcanet Press, Manchester, 2006.

Kaplan, R. D., *Balkan Ghosts: A Journey through History*, Picador, London, 2005.

Kitchen, M., *A History of Modern Germany, 1800–2000*, Blackwell Publishing, Oxford, 2006.

Koster, E. A. (ed.), *The Physical Geography of Western Europe* (Oxford Regional Environments), Oxford University Press, Oxford, 2005.

McGiffen, S. P., *The European Union: A Critical Guide*, Pluto Press, London, 2006.

Morley, D. and Robins, K. (eds.), *British Cultural Studies: Geography, Nationality and Identity*, Oxford University Press, Oxford, 2005.

Official Directory of the European Union 2006–2007, European Communities, Luxembourg, 2006.

Ostergren, R. C. and J. G. Rice, *The Europeans: A Geography of People, Culture, and Environment*, The Guilford Press, New York, 2004.

Sassoon, D., *Contemporary Italy: Politics, Economy and Society since 1945* (2nd edn.), Addison Wesley Longman, London, 1997.

Wilson, A., *The Ukrainians: Unexpected Nation* (2nd edn.), Yale University Press, New Haven, CT, 2002.

Woodhouse, C. M., *Modern Greece: A Short History* (5th edn.), Faber & Faber, London, 2000.

General Web Sites

www.ethnologue.com
A comprehensive guide to all the languages of the world.

www.factmonster.com/ipka/A0770414.html
Geography facts and figures for kids.

www.geographic.org
Information on geography for students, teachers, parents and children.

www.odci.gov/cia/publications/factbook/index.html
Central Intelligence Agency factbook of country profiles.

www.panda.org
World Wide Fund for Nature (WWF).

www.peoplegroups.org/default.aspx
Listing and information on major ethnic groups around the world.

www.worldatlas.com
A world atlas of facts, flags and maps.

INDEX